Blackpool

The Glory Years Remembered

Blackpool

The Glory Years Remembered

Mike Prestage

The Breedon Books
Publishing Company
Derby

First published in Great Britain in 2000 by
The Breedon Books Publishing Company Limited
Breedon House, 3 The Parker Centre, Derby, DE21 4SZ.

ISBN 1 85983 198 2

Printed and bound by Butler & Tanner Ltd., Selwood Printing Works,
Caxton Road, Frome, Somerset.

Colour separations and jacket printing by
GreenShires Group Ltd., Leicester.

Contents

Acknowledgements
To all ex-players
and long-time supporters
of Blackpool Football Club
who took the time to share their memories.

Introduction

WITH World War Two at an end but the austerity it had brought with it lingering on for some years yet, the people of Britain wanted entertainment and the coastal resort of Blackpool was among those happy to oblige. Blackpool was as famous then as it is now, for its brash and breezy image, a fun place to visit with the Tower and the Golden Mile. Yet in the late 1940s and throughout the 1950s, it was equally famous for its football team. Not least because their international-studded line-up included Stanley Matthews, a genius of a player who can lay strong claim to being England's greatest-ever footballer.

During those years, Blackpool were a dominant force in English football and yet it can be argued that they never achieved the glory their talents deserved. There is no doubt, though, that the cultured football they played won admiration far beyond the town's boundaries. They were to play in three FA Cup Finals in five years and finish as Football League championship runners-up in 1956. Two of those Wembley Finals have entered the folklore of the competition. The first, in 1948 when they lost to Manchester United, is widely regarded as one of the greatest football exhibitions witnessed at the Twin Towers. The third, in 1953, has entered the annals as the 'Matthews' Final', when the Wizard of Dribble inspired the side to a dramatic comeback against Bolton Wanderers to win the trophy 4-3.

This was an era which brings back memories of sportsmanship and fair play that appear to have been lost to the modern game, although make no mistake, there were many hard and uncompromising players about. It was a time that pre-dated satellite television coverage, corporate hospitality and players living the millionaire lifestyles of Hollywood film stars. There was little time, either, for all the histrionics indulged in by today's players. And for all the hype surrounding the 21st-century Premiership, the post-war years were a time when 40 million people poured through the turnstiles each year – twice the number who watch League football today.

The importance of the football team to Blackpool was made clear after losing the 1951 Final, when they were beaten by Newcastle United 2-0. Before the war the Seasiders were never a major force in English football and spent most of their early history in the Second Division. Now at a dinner at the Winter Gardens to celebrate reaching the Final, the club's chairman, Harry Evans, said that a dream which had been dismissed as impossible had come true. Blackpool had established themselves as the 'Arsenal of the North'. The club had emulated the success of the team with the biggest support in the country at that time.

During the 1950-51 season, some 1,001,407 people watched the first team in League games outside Blackpool and a further 401,775 watched their Cup-ties. Few teams in the country could rival them as such a box office draw beyond their own boundaries. Indeed, for many clubs the visit of Blackpool with the legendary Stanley Matthews attracted the biggest attendance of the season. Wherever they went they were an advertisement not only for football but also for the town. The publicity value could not be calculated and in the dark days of winter it brought people, who would not otherwise visit, into the town for football. The visitors are still flocking to the resort today, but sadly it is no longer the football team that is a major draw.

At the same Winter Gardens dinner, another subject was raised that is being tackled only today. There was a call for a new 50,000-capacity stadium more in keeping with the club's new status. It was said to be a long-term project, but surely few tucking into the dinner back in 1951 could have imagined that it would be the new millennium before the redevelopment of the stadium was undertaken. Ironically, the need for such a large capacity has, of course, become redundant over the decades.

Another key factor in the rise of Blackpool as a football team was closely linked to the town's attraction as a tourist resort. Put simply, Blackpool was a very desirable location to live and a fun place for young football players to socialise. The maximum wage benefited the club because, given that everybody was on the same wage, standard of living became an important draw. It was only once the wages ceiling was removed in the early 1960s that the club's fortunes began to suffer. Then the big city clubs had the cash to counter the allure of bracing sea air.

The importance to the football club of the attraction of the town was underlined in an article in the *Evening Gazette* in February 1953, on the eve of a fifth-round FA Cup tie against Southampton. This was the Cup-winning season but what the correspondent noted was that the two clubs last met in the competition 29 years before. Five of the players from that match in 1924 were still living in the town and the writer was left to reflect on what a magnet to professional footballers Blackpool was, and that once they arrived they rarely wanted to leave. True to his words, many of the players from the club's greatest era in the post-war years can still be found in and around the town.

One such player is Hugh Kelly, who played 468 League and Cup games for the club between 1946 and 1960. He was signed from local side Jeanfield Swifts in his native Perth in 1943 and recalls: "Blackpool was well known in Scotland because it was a popular holiday resort and I had heard so much about the place. Everybody I knew had been there on holiday and although I had already had trials with Glasgow Celtic and Motherwell, I was pleased with the chance to move down south. I was approached by a well-known scout called Vic Hamilton, who sent half a dozen players from Scotland over a period of a few years. As well as the £10 signing on fee, I was promised a holiday for two anywhere in England, but that never materialised. From first arriving I loved Blackpool. Everything about the place pleased me so much. As I took my first tram ride along the front I thought it was the loveliest town I had ever been in. Playing for Blackpool and living in the town fulfilled my ambition."

He added: "The post-war years were a great time for football. There was huge support across the country and the standard of football was very good. There were a lot of very good players and teams and it was a privilege to be playing for Blackpool and against the best of the clubs and their top players. I think the records speak for themselves at Blackpool. We had a very good side from the resumption of the League in 1946 and right the way through to the 1960s. Generally it was good, season after good season."

Kelly recognises there are key differences between his day and the modern game. The pace of the game today is so much quicker and the formations and tactics are different. The basic footballing skills are the same, though, and he feels the great players of his era would be able to compete in the modern game. Discipline on the pitch was much better when he played with referees exercising far more power. He remembers flare-ups between players on the field were extremely rare.

Scottish international Allan Brown, who played when Blackpool were at the height of their powers during the 1950s, remembers the closeness that existed between players and fans that he believes is lost from the modern game. After training the players used to have a cup of tea at a hut near the stand where the fans would call in and chat about football. Many of the players caught the tram to the ground and could mingle with the supporters before the game. There was no sense of superiority among the players. They were a part of the community along with the people who paid to watch them. It is all a far cry from modern players and their showbusiness lifestyles and earnings that provide an affluent way of life well apart from those who help pay their inflated salaries.

He wryly adds, though, that while in his days the players listened to the advice given by fans, they rarely ever took it.

He also enjoyed his stay in Blackpool, not just because of the standard of the football but also the attractions of the town itself. After his playing days,like many others he retired to the resort. He says: "I had some good times at Blackpool. It was a good place to live and then retire to. There were always strong showbiz connections between the club and the main attractions. We could get to see the best shows at the Winter Gardens and meet the stars. I saw Bob Hope down there once. Somebody sorted out tickets for us and we were always made welcome."

Syd Bevers was a founding member of the Atomic Boys, a troupe of supporters dressed in tangerine and white suits and straw hats, as well as fancy-dress outfits, who followed the Seasiders everywhere. He remembers football was hugely popular after the war and nowhere more so than Blackpool where both the town and football club were on the crest of a wave. The players were local heroes, but were also approachable. He recalls organising a fund-raising dance in the Tower Ball Room in 1949 and the place was hired for £100. It was a sell out and a major reason was that Stanley Matthews had donated a dinner service for the raffle and then agreed to present the prize in person. He also helped sell the tickets for the event.

Now 85, Bevers reveals the strong links between the club and the town's tourism. The Atomic Boys acquired the role of official mascots, but he says many of the stunts they performed had been carefully orchestrated with the town's publicity department. They were seen as an important marketing tool and provided with leaflets and brochures promoting the town, which they handed out on their travels. They also got complimentary match tickets. In the days before public relations was a multi-million pound business engaged in by all commercial organisations, the Blackpool council was ahead of its day.

He recalls: "Before the 1953 Cup Final the town's publicity department sent for me. They had come up with an idea where they wanted two or three of the Atomic Boys to push me around London on a rickshaw they had arranged to borrow from Elstree Studios. After some discussion it was decided against the idea because they thought the rickshaw might get broken if Bolton fans decided to overturn it as a prank. Instead I took a giant stick of Blackpool rock with the words 'Sir Winston Churchill' lettered through it and delivered it to Number 10 Downing Street. I was in there about 20 minutes. Everybody thought I would get arrested when I walked up and knocked on the door. It was a wonderful occasion. Although the

Prime Minister happened to be out, officials still took the stick of rock. All the newspapers carried the story. Such gimmicks were in keeping with the image of Blackpool as a fun place."

Bill Perry played through the club's greatest era and he has no doubt that 'it was the best time to be playing football'. There were drawbacks, of course. The maximum wage limited the earnings of a player and from the playing point of view the pitches were not of the quality which modern players take for granted. He recalls that Blackpool used to train on the same Bloomfield Road pitch that they played League and Cup games on each Saturday, which certainly didn't help. Even in the 1950s, the lack of any training facilities at Blackpool was unusual. Most League sides had at least an extra training pitch they could use midweek to protect the playing surface at the stadium. Others had gym facilities and indoor training grounds. Not at Blackpool where investment in infrastructure, so commonplace during the decade throughout the rest of the League, passed Blackpool by.

"Often, particularly towards the end of the season, the centre of the pitch was reduced to a quagmire," reflects Perry. "Playing with the old leather ball didn't help because it became very heavy. The standard of play couldn't be quite as good as today where the facilities are so much better and the modern plastic ball so much lighter and easier to control. I envy the players today with the perfect pitches and lighter boots and pads."

He laments the decline in discipline among players compared with his day when the referee's word was law. The money may be a lot more and the pressures greater for the modern player but he still thinks they have a role model image to project and many of them fail to do so. He also thinks that the maximum wage had the benefit of rewarding every player. Football is a team game and he believes the defender deserves as much as the forward whose role may ensure that he has a higher profile and can nowadays command a higher salary.

He added: "If I was playing and was the best on the field, I would still not like to think that a team-mate was earning less than me. I'm surprised that they all put up with it. I think it just leads to some animosity in the dressing-room that was absent in my day. Stanley

Matthews put up with a maximum wage for virtually all his career. At times he might have felt he was worth more money, but knowing Stan he wouldn't begrudge anybody earning the same as him. Certainly I never remember hearing about him arguing for more for himself."

He thinks many of the modern players are overrated. David Beckham, for Manchester United and England, has excellent vision and can deliver accurate crosses, but he struggles to beat a man. Stan Matthews and Ernie Taylor had all three skills. What would be their value in the modern game? He regrets the lost skill of the winger, for as he says: "The crowd love to see a winger taking a defender on, beating him and getting crosses into the penalty area where something is bound to happen if you can keep doing it consistently. That was what they loved to see Stan doing. When he got the ball, nine out of ten times he took it up the wing. He was so successful at beating his man that the rest of the forwards would just head towards the goalmouth, assuming a cross was coming over. That was how good Stan was."

Francis Charlesworth, chairman of the Blackpool Supporters' Association, remembers being taken as a small child to Bloomfield Road and being allowed to sit on the wall and watch the last games of some of the great players of the golden era performing in the famous tangerine shirts. There was George Farm in goal and Bill Perry on the wing and, of course, the incomparable Matthews.

"I remember these were the players my father always talked about. I knew little about football, but I can remember seeing Matthews stepping one way and then the other and leaving a defender on his backside. I seriously got involved when I was a bit older and by then the club was on the slide but it is good to have the memories of the greats to recall. As a small child I can remember being taken aback by the tremendous atmosphere and the huge crowd of people. There were 30,000 gates then."

He believes in the halcyon days of football after the war the maximum wage, and the transfer market being much quieter, meant players were content to stay at one club. It instilled a sense of loyalty that is missing in the modern game. On the Monday after a game, the players would be out and about in the town and if they had a bad game somebody would tell them. He feels modern players have become untouchable. They know nothing of the supporters and, he suspects, care even less.

Peter Collins didn't sit on the wall to see the game when his father took him during the war years. They took a stool with them and he stood on that. He remembers seeing Saturday games and, when he could play truant from school, the midweek games as well. On a derelict piece of land next to the ground was a green hut that served as a café where fans and players would mix during the week. And when he was old enough to go alone he would arrive early and join in an impromptu kickabout with other lads before the gates were opened and they would all flood in to get a prime spot and a good view. In the East Paddock, where he went, there was no concrete terracing, just ash and shale. As he got older he graduated to the Spion Kop. This was the great Blackpool side in its heyday and, looking back on those wonderful times, he realises as youngsters they never properly appreciated just how good the side was.

The man who has not only supported the club for a lifetime, but also worked on the administration side for many years and still has a part-time role, said: "There were some great players. Stan Matthews, Ernie Taylor, who arrived after the Final against Newcastle, and Stan Mortensen, Bill Perry and Allan Brown. It was a terrific forward line. If we were on top and winning, they used to turn the last 20 minutes into an exhibition. It was superb football. If they went behind it would be Harry Johnston at the back who would lead by example and lift the whole side. He was a great unsung hero. It was wonderful as a child being there and watching them in action"

He believes that a factor in the rise of a great Blackpool side after the war was the fact that the town was close to a number of wartime RAF bases. Many players guested for the club during the war years and got to know the town. Their success helped put the football team on the map because Blackpool were one of the leading sides in football during the war years. Some of these players were enticed back when hostilities ended and they returned to their own clubs. Stanley Matthews was the most famous, but there were others. Once back in the resort, there were also business opportunities to run alongside their playing careers. Matthews owned a hotel for a while. Kelly had a shop and a business making ice-cream.

Much has changed since those heady days and not always for the best. He said: "The game today is a lot different to those days. Now they are better coached and the game is a lot faster. I think nowadays it is more like having a game of chess with the tactics and the strategies. For the average fan, though, I don't think they get the same excitement now as we did and there isn't the feeling for football and the local team that there used to be. I'm not saying the football itself is better or worse. With five forwards and not too much protection for the goalkeeper, there was a lot more attacking and a lot more action in the old days."

Recapturing the spirit that the club once generated in the town is not easy when they are languishing, for now at least, in the lowest division. "I now have the job of marketing Blackpool FC and it is a battle. You walk around the town and see people wearing football shirts of other teams. It doesn't look right. Because we are at the bottom, it is no longer fashionable for the youngsters to support their local side. Television has given a huge exposure to the Premiership sides. Nobody is interested in how good we were. The kids can't grasp the idea that Blackpool were the Manchester United of their day and they had some of the greatest players. At one stage every player was at least a 'B' international and most were full internationals. Of course, we never had replica shirts when I went down, it was rosettes, scarves and rattles."

Like most young boys in the town, Ray Hall was first taken to Bloomfield Road by his father. It was soon after League football resumed in the 1940s. The first game he can remember was against Charlton Athletic, and Sam Bartram was in goal. He remembers the atmosphere and the excitement. His father had first started going to see the Seasiders in the 1920s and it remained the workingman's game. It was a cheap afternoon for the two of them. Later he would be on the books at Blackpool and play in the lower sides.

Yet he never wanted to be a professional footballer. It was partly because he preferred playing with his mates in a local side in an amateur league. But also because he had seen through the glamour of being a full-time player and knew the reality of a pro's life. "In the mid-1950s players were only on £14 a week and many would be washed up and on the scrapheap by the time they were in their early 30s. Then they would end up selling their medals. For too many young players hoping to make it in the game, their future was on Skid Row. There were still some great memories, though. I remember training with Stan Mortensen in the last year of his career and even at 35 he was electric. He inspired you. I also quickly knew that I would be wasting my time thinking there was a playing future at Blackpool. Virtually everyone was an international. It was incredible."

This was the time when the cream of the country's players wanted to be at Blackpool. The old adage that a successful team can always attract top players was certainly true. There was also the chance to be by the sea and, as Hall points out, it beat living in a city like Manchester or Birmingham. There were also a lot of Scottish players attracted to the town.

He added: "It was not just the great players in our side. There were some wonderful sides that visited Bloomfield Road and we saw players like Duncan Edwards, John Charles and Raich Carter. Some of the games were pure magic. Some of the most famous footballers in the world have been through the old players' entrance at the ground. When they were knocking it down as part of the improvements, I went and took a picture just to bring back the memories. It was probably football's greatest era and we were a key part of it."

Hall believes there was a higher level of skill in those days and he blames modern coaches and schools of excellence for taking the flair out of young players. He thinks many of today's players lack the basics and he despairs of hearing of professional players who can't use both feet. He has no doubts that the greats he watched in the golden days of football would be able to compete in the modern game.

Blackpool's fortunes may have suffered since the golden era and many younger fans must roll their eyes skywards at the mention of players who had retired long before they were born. No doubt it is hard for those not there to comprehend the awe in which the Blackpool side was held throughout the land. Spending too much time looking backwards is never constructive and, of course, there are hopes that the foundations for a brighter future are being put in place. Yet it is equally unwise to ignore the past. The following chapters will hopefully bring back nostalgic memories for those of a certain age and give a valuable insight to others of one of the greatest clubs in English post-war football.

Football Returns

WITH the war over, League football resumed in 1946 and, as though frozen in time, the fixture list that had been suspended after three games in 1939 was revived. Blackpool had made a superb start to the pre-war campaign with three wins that saw the side at the top of the First Division for the first time in the club's history. For the fans the question was whether that success story be repeated. And there were hopes that if it could, the club's pre-eminence would last far more than three games. Only time would tell, but they were exciting times to be heading down to Bloomfield Road.

It was not just at Blackpool that football was booming. Across the country people were flocking to League grounds as a nation starved of proper competitive football welcomed back the great entertainment of the masses. The biggest crowd before which the Blackpool players would perform was at Goodison Park in April 1947 when 63,617 were there to follow the action. Just over 17,000 had been at Bloomfield Road in 1939 for the visit of Wolves. Seven years on, the corresponding fixture now saw 27,623 standing on the terraces and sitting in the stands. Rationing was still in place and, for many, times were hard, but football provided a cheap day out. For many of the players it was a welcome chance to be back in action after losing so many of their best years to the hostilities.

Although players had been guesting for other clubs during the war, all now returned to their original teams for the eagerly-awaited return of League football. For the 1938-39 season, Blackpool had spent over £60,000 on new players and the fans were eager to see them back in action having only had the briefest glimpse of them before the war.

There was a keen sense of anticipation. For much of their history up to World War Two, Blackpool were a side that struggled in the Second Division. Although the Seasiders had entered the Football League in the final years of the 19th century, it was 1930 before they first graced the top division and it was hardly an auspicious entry. They were twice 20th before being relegated in 1932-33. However, the appointment of Joe Smith as manager in 1935 proved the catalyst for the success that would see the Blackpool team become a major force in the late 1940s and throughout the 1950s. The team had won promotion in 1936-37, and with the new players they threatened to make their mark.

Not all of the players expected to return did so, despite an edict from the Football League. Jock Dodds had been signed from Sheffield United for £10,500 and quickly showed his goalscoring prowess, netting three times in the three games before the outbreak of war ended League football. He had also been a goalscoring machine in wartime football, setting some incredible records. He scored 30 times in 18 appearances, including seven in an 11-2 demolition of Oldham Athletic in the first regional league in 1939-40. During the war years he scored over 200 goals, with the highlights being eight against Stockport County and seven against Tranmere, including a hat-trick in under three minutes. It is a record he doubts will be broken because the kissing and cuddling that marks a goal in the modern era means the clock would have run down before they restarted the match. Dodds was also the last man to score a hat-trick for Scotland against England.

During the war, Blackpool, aided by Dodds and some star names who guested for the club during this time including, of course, Stanley Matthews, tasted success as probably the most powerful side in English football at this time. They won the Northern Section of the regional league on three occasions, had a triumph in the Lanca-shire Cup and twice reached the War Cup Final, beating Sheffield Wednesday 2-1 in a replay after drawing at Bloomfield Road 2-2 in 1943 and the following year losing 4-1 away to Aston Villa. As

Northern winners of the Cup they travelled to Stamford Bridge to meet Arsenal, winners of the Southern War Cup, and won 4-2 in front of a crowd of more than 55,000.

Dodds, though, was not to return after the war ended. Fifty years on the player reveals: "After the war there were reduced wages of £7 in summer and £5 in winter. I told them they would be looking for a new centre-forward. I had lost some of the best years of my career and had been turning out for Blackpool when they were getting 30,000 crowds for wartime matches and I was serving as an RAF sergeant physical training instructor and getting £1 10s [£1.50] to play. The last contract I signed was before the war and although the FA said you had to go back, I went to Shamrock Rovers. The Irish club could sign anybody and I was offered £20 a week, which was big money, and a £1,500 signing on fee as well. Blackpool's problem was they earned big money, but they didn't like to part with any of it."

The player had asked himself the same question that many of his generation posed. Where did all the money go? With massive crowds and low wages, a lot of money was being generated in football and one thing all performing in the post-war years knew for sure was that the players were not getting it. Many shared Dodd's sense of injustice. Unlike him, few were able to do anything about it other than vent their spleen to other professionals and hope for a more equitable situation one day.

It was not just at club level where the players got a raw deal. He remembers after an international match for Scotland there was a knock at the door and one of his team-mates was called to see the secretary. He had submitted £5 expenses and when they were queried he said the reason for the figure was that he had brought his wife. "We picked you, we didn't pick your wife," was the reply. Dodds said: "On that day we had played England before 133,000 people at Hampden Park. How much money did that crowd generate? That was how ridiculous it was in those days that they could quibble over a player's expenses when it was such a small amount involved."

He returned to League football in November 1946 and joined

Everton, where his goalscoring touch had not deserted him, scoring 36 goals in 55 League games. He ended his career with Lincoln City. On his retirement he returned to Blackpool where he went into business running a chain of betting shops and then an hotel. He has no regrets about heading for Ireland rather than accept the terms being dictated to him. The vast majority of players got a raw deal at this time with the clubs holding all the power. Jock Dodds was not one of them.

Blackpool might have been without Dodds, but they still emulated the start they had made in 1939, winning their opening three games against Huddersfield Town, Brentford and Wolves. A goalscorer in each of the matches was a player who would become a legend not just in the tangerine jersey of Blackpool, but also in the white shirt of England. Stan Mortensen had announced his arrival in League football in dramatic fashion.

Huddersfield proved to be easier opponents than might have been expected and the longer the game went on the more comfortable the home defence was, although the Yorkshire side were to rue some missed chances early on. While not reading too much into the result, there was a general feeling that Blackpool would certainly be able to compete at this level in the new campaign. Already Mortensen was making his mark, and the forwards generally had a class which their opponents lacked. Three goals was the reward with just one for Town. It was a satisfactory reintroduction to League football after such a long absence.

Mortensen had an enviable record as a centre-forward and he was a player feared by opposing defences during the ten years he played for Blackpool. Although not large in stature, he was quick and powerful and 222 goals for the Seasiders in 354 League and Cup appearances was proof positive of his goalscoring prowess. In his 25 appearances for the national side he scored 23 goals. His England debut came in May 1947 when he scored four goals against Portugal. Mortensen was the perfect partner for Stanley Matthews and the two complemented each other perfectly at both club and international level, Matthews' accurate crosses being met by one of the game's deadliest finishers.

Mortensen was playing local football in his native South Shields when Blackpool signed him in May 1938 and after early doubts about his ability were dispelled, thanks to a punishing training regime, he was working his way through the lower teams at Bloomfield Road when war intervened. He played for the Seasiders in wartime football as well as other clubs. By the resumption of League football he was first-team centre-forward and would remain so until his departure to Hull City late in 1955. He was the club's top goalscorer in each of those seasons. After Hull, his playing career took him to Southport, Bath City and Lancaster City. He continued to live in Blackpool and for a spell in the late 1960s managed the club. By a curious irony his death in May 1991 was on the very day the club were back at Wembley for the first time since the Cup Final in 1953. The occasion, though, was far removed from Blackpool's glory days. They lost to Torquay United on penalties in a Fourth Division Play-off Final.

Back in 1946-47, eight wins in their first ten games had raised hopes that the side might be challenging for the title, but a slump that began with a 4-2 defeat at the hands of Sheffield United at Bramall Lane saw them win only once in six games. Thereafter there were too many reverses to make a realistic challenge and Blackpool finished fifth. It still represented the best League placing in the club's history and boded well for the future. Mortensen had scored 28 goals and underlined that he was a proven goalscorer at the highest level. Low points were two 5-0 defeats at Bloomfield Road, against Middlesbrough and Sunderland. Such reverses aside, the portents were good for the future.

Hugh Kelly recalls that there was a great spirit in the camp with some real characters, which made being at Blackpool a great experience for more than just the performances being produced on the field. One anecdote he relates concerns goalkeeper Jock Wallace and Mortensen. "Jock was a great one for practical jokes and larking about. He was a big, jovial type of chap. He also had hands like a shovel. I remember being in the bath and Stan was on the edge and Jock gave him such a slap across his backside Morty finished up in the pool with everybody laughing. Later Morty returned in just a shirt and feigned being angry, saying he would sort it out with Jock. The goalkeeper just laughed and tipped a load of water over him. Morty warned him not to do it again or else, so he threw more at him and told him: 'You've gone and got your shirt all wet.' Morty just laughed and said: 'No I haven't. I put your shirt on.' They were both great blokes and there was always laughing and joking. It was a great club to be involved with."

During the late 1940s, Blackpool would rely on players who had been the product of Joe Smith's building programme at the club that was disrupted by hostilities. In all, eight players who appeared in the Blackpool side in the last full season in 1938-39 would figure in the new campaign. They included Wallace and Willie Buchan, an inside-forward signed from Celtic for £10,000 in 1938. Two of the half-back line were to prove experienced campaigners in the Blackpool cause through the late 1940s and into the early 1950s after both making their debuts in the 1937-38 season. Harry Johnston and Eric Hayward would be joined by George Farrow in one of the most revered half-back lines in English football. These were players who had lost the best years of their careers to the war and were determined to enjoy what was left.

Despite losing seven years of League football, Harry Johnston still managed to pack much into his Blackpool career, proving himself the model of consistency. Matthews once described him as forceful and direct. He played 438 League and Cup matches for the club and three times captained the side in Wembley Cup Finals. He was at Bloomfield Road man and boy, having joined the groundstaff when he was 15. He made his debut three years later, against Preston North End, and quickly established himself in the first team. A key player at the heart of the defence, he played in all three half-back positions and could turn his hand to centre-forward if the need arose. His leadership qualities were reflected in his many years as captain of a star-studded side. He won ten caps for England and that total would have been far higher but for the presence of the great Billy Wright. Recognition of his undoubted talent came in 1950-51 when he was voted Footballer of the Year. In 1955 he left Bloomfield Road to become manager at Reading, although he returned 12 years later as chief scout. Along with Matthews and Mortensen he was one of the commanding presences in a great Blackpool side.

Eric Hayward was the unsung hero of the half-back line, yet his contribution was immense in the early years after the war. He was born in Newcastle under Lyme in 1917 and had played for Hanley and Port Vale before arriving at Bloomfield Road in 1937. He played some wartime football, although service in India limited the games he played. A solid performer in defence, he appeared in both the 1948 and 1951 Finals and was to play nearly 300 League and Cup games for the club until 1952. He returned as assistant manager to Ron Suart in the late 1950s.

Playing alongside them was George Farrow, who could consider himself unlucky to have missed out on Blackpool's Wembley date in 1948. Farrow had arrived at Bloomfield Road from Bournemouth in 1936 and quickly made his debut in a home win against West Ham United. A tough tackler, his presence helped win promotion in his first season and he was a regular up to the war. He would stay for 13 seasons and many considered him unlucky not to win international honours. His sale to Sheffield United four months before the Cup Final deprived him of the chance to show his skills on that most famous stage.

The final piece in the jigsaw that would see Blackpool become a major force in the game for the next decade was put into place in the close season. When the Blackpool team ran out to face Chelsea at Bloomfield Road on August 23, in their opening match of the season, the number-seven shirt was worn by Stanley Matthews. He had been signed from Stoke City for £11,500 and was keen to return to the town and the club, which he had got to know during the war years when he was stationed nearby and guested for the Seasiders. Already an established international, he would be an irrepressible presence on the flank for the club. Now the glory days were about to dawn for Blackpool. However, the 1947-48 campaign would not see the side making a great impression in the League. This was to be the year Cup fever came to Blackpool and the first visit to Wembley to contest a Cup Final.

On the
Wembley Trail

THE team that Joe Smith had assembled came up trumps in 1948 with a trip to Wembley to contest an FA Cup Final that was to enter football folklore as one of the best games witnessed at the Twin Towers. Often, nerves and the pressure of the occasion can nullify hopes of seeing good football. This time, though, the players rose to the challenge and the pre-match hype was well justified. Blackpool lost the game 4-2 to Manchester United, but they succeeded in bringing pride to their home town and were given a heroes' welcome on their return.

The footballing fates had been kind with the draw in the early rounds and Blackpool made sure there were no silly slips to ruin the chance of a trip to Wembley. In the first four rounds the Seasiders scored 15 goals and didn't concede any. It was an impressive passage to the semi-final, whatever the limitations of some of the opposition. With each round successfully completed, hopes rose in the town that this would be their year.

First up on January 10 were Leeds United, then a lowly second Division side, and nearly 5,000 people made the journey from Yorkshire to Bloomfield Road. In the build-up to the game the stands were sold out and there were only paddock tickets available priced 3s (15p) and 4s 6d (23p). Blackpool were strong favourites, but given the club's woeful record in the Cup, few were tempting fate with overconfidence. Between the wars the Seasiders had suffered some embarrassing defeats. They travelled to both Southport and

Southend and lost each time. They suffered reverses on their own ground to lowly opposition like Watford, Swansea Town, Oldham Athletic and Luton Town.

Leeds were having a poor season, yet Blackpool's preparations were far from ideal. Their Scottish goalkeeper, Jock Wallace, shocked the club and its fans by failing to report for training in the week prior to the Cup-tie. He wrote, making clear he would not be playing and he wished the team all the best for the match. His absence was due to a dispute with the club, which was not resolved to his satisfaction.

It was the first game Wallace had missed for Blackpool since the resumption of League football the previous season. He had been at the club for 14 years since joining from Raith Rovers in March 1934. He was an outstanding goalkeeper and was as famed for his bravery as his agility. A serious injury at Plymouth in December 1936 was feared to have ended his playing career, yet incredibly he was back within five weeks and helping Blackpool to promotion. In all he played 250 League and Cup games for the Seasiders. Within a month of the Leeds dispute he was sold to injury-hit Derby County for a nominal fee of £500 and helped the Rams to the Cup semi-final that year, where they lost to Manchester United. If he had stayed at Blackpool he would have gone one better, but it was not to be. After helping Derby out in their goalkeeping crisis he left at the end of the season and finished his career at Leith Athletic.

For the Leeds tie, his place in the Blackpool goal was taken by Joe Robinson, who had been signed from Hartlepool United in the summer of 1946. He faced a Leeds side that worked hard in attack but were unable to seriously threaten and the home defenders made the goalkeeper's job as easy as it could be. At the other end, the muddy conditions could not bog down Stanley Matthews, and the other forwards also showed enterprise. There were four goals for the home crowd to celebrate with Willie McIntosh getting a brace and one apiece for Stan Mortensen and George Dick.

There was again a home draw and again lower League opposition for the fourth round when Third Division North Chester were the visitors. The only fears beforehand were that thick frost on the pitch would prove a leveller. Extra trains and a fleet of 60 coaches were laid on for the visiting fans and they helped ensure a healthy 26,419 attendance. Chester supporters' hopes were quickly dashed with a goal for the home side after seven minutes, scored by Eddie Shimwell. It was a bizarre goal and a personal nightmare for Chester goalkeeper George Scales. A 60-yard clearance took an awkward bounce on the frozen pitch and sailed over the goalkeeper's head. In the 25th minute, Mortensen was on target and, barring a miracle, for Chester it was all over. In the second half, goals for Mortensen and Harry Johnston gave the victory a comfortable gloss.

Colchester United, then a non-League club, were the visitors for the fifth round and Cup fever was attracting interest not just in the town. Special stands had to be built for five newsreel companies who wanted to capture the day's events on celluloid and the BBC's fledgeling television service was also filming the match for a broadcast in the London area on Saturday night. It was a very early predecessor of BBC's *Match of the Day* programme.

The Essex team stayed at the South Promenade hotel owned by Stanley Matthews. It no doubt gave the players the chance to see in close-up their likely nemesis come the day of the match. The United player-manager Ted Fenton had drawn up an 'M' plan as his tactic to ensure a Cup upset in the best spirit of the competition. The masterstroke involved stopping Matthews and Mortensen. It would prove far easier said than done. Certainly the pundits were not overly impressed, making Colchester United the 100-1 outsiders for the Cup.

The Colchester supporters began arriving at 4am on the Saturday of the match and were reported to be confident of success. Before 7am, the queues were 100 yards long outside cafés and everywhere there was the blue and white colours of their team on banners, rosettes and top hats. Colchester had already beaten First Division Huddersfield Town and so giant-killing was nothing new. Fenton predicted that the football world might be in for a shock.

With the Bloomfield Road pitch cloying and heavy, the home defenders resisted Colchester pressure in the first half-hour and then, as the visitors tired, the Blackpool forwards began to take advantage. Five goals were the reward, with two each for Mortensen and McIntosh while Alec Munro scored one. The United players tried to play football throughout and never resorted to illegal tactics to keep in contention. Afterwards they were praised for their sportsmanship and assured they had not disgraced themselves. In a nice touch, a celebration dinner was held for the two teams at a local hotel, attended by civic dignitaries. The menu included a sack of oysters presented to the Mayor of Blackpool on behalf of the Colchester Corporation.

In the sixth round, Blackpool were on the road for the first time in the competition with a tie against either Fulham or Everton. Such was the demand for tickets, the Bloomfield Road offices were besieged with applications even though it was impossible to do anything until the opposition was known and details of the allocation had been realised. Everton would mean First Division opposition for the first time, but for the fans less distance to travel and more chance of getting a ticket with Goodison Park capable of holding more than 60,000 fans.

In the event, the tie was settled in Second Division Fulham's favour and it was to London the Blackpool team and their supporters had to travel. The inclusion of Walter Rickett at outside-left in place of Alec Munro meant the first change in the Blackpool FA Cup team. The Fulham players had enjoyed a day out at Brighton as part of their preparations for the match. For the Seasiders this was the biggest Cup game since they lost a famous quarter-final against Blackburn Rovers at Ewood Park in 1925. If they progressed it would be into uncharted territory for the club.

At 4am, the Atomic Boys were on the first special train out of Blackpool, carrying a four-feet high cartoon bearing the words 'Up the 'Pool. What about the M Plan?', and thousands of others followed. The 'M' Plan, of course, referred to the famous forward line of the day, most of whose players' names all began with the letter 'M': Matthews, Munro, Mortensen and McIntosh. A large crowd of supporters went to the team's hotel with rattles and bells to make their support heard. The rest of the residents might not have been too pleased, but everybody was left in no doubt that Blackpool were in town for the Cup. There were fans dressed in tangerine and white suits, and one man had fitted a brass funnel to a pair of bellows so it sounded like a ship's siren wailing. For those left behind, the *Evening Gazette* was forced to print a plea for desperate fans not to ring the newspaper's offices during the match because the switchboard was in danger of being swamped.

While the more pessimistic fans were hoping for a draw and a replay at Bloomfield Road, most were confident that Blackpool could settle the tie at the first time of asking and, despite the lottery nature of the FA Cup, their team, on paper at least, had by far the greater pedigree. The conditions were ideal for good football and it was now up to the players to perform. And perform they did. The final score was 2-0, but it could have been a bigger margin while Joe Robinson in the visitors' net was virtually a spectator. Blackpool were always driving forward while the Fulham forwards struggled to make any headway. Admittedly, their cause was not helped by being reduced to ten men for three-quarters of the match through an injury to Harry Freeman. To their credit, the Fulham defenders never gave up the battle although they were outclassed. Mortensen collected the first and McIntosh the second and there should have been a few more.

A gypsy fortune-teller on the Golden Mile had confidently predicted a Cup Final between Blackpool and Spurs before the competition started and her reading of the runes had been seized on by supporters looking for all the positive omens they could find. Now, though, the draw for the semi-final conspired to scupper the prophecy. The two sides would meet in the penultimate round at Villa Park, Birmingham. It was, gypsy predictions apart, a good draw for Blackpool. Spurs were another Second Division side and the Seasiders had accounted for two of those already. It also kept them away from the tournament favourites, Manchester United. If Blackpool could win, they would have reached Wembley without meeting a First Division club.

The two sides had met in the Cup only once before and it was not a game for Blackpool supporters to recall with fond memories. They lost 6-1 in 1913. Yet those in the biggest exodus for a football match in the town's history were not going to have their confidence dented by such historic precedents. Nearly 10,000 supporters made the journey on a fleet of 300 coaches, and a further 4,000 travelled on special trains.

History was not going to repeat itself and this time it was a very different story. Before a crowd of 67,500, a Mortensen hat-trick ensured he maintained his record of scoring in every round and that the Seasiders were Wembley-bound. It was, though, a close-run thing. With four minutes of the game to go, Spurs were leading, thanks to a goal by Len Duquemin, although for most of the match he had been involved in a good contest with Hugh Kelly. The first-half goal came during a moment's loss of concentration in the Blackpool defence and the highly-regarded centre-forward profited from the confusion. Yet when Mortensen burst through the Spurs defence to fire home, it was the Lancashire side who had wrested control from the Londoners and who were clear favourites when the match went into extra-time. Two more goals were the reward and for the fans who were there this will always be 'Mortensen's match'.

Now the race for a Cup Final ticket was on. The supporters' cause was not helped by the decision of the FA Council to reduce the number of tickets made available to the two Finalists from 25,000 to around only 12,000, to meet the requests of the 88 League clubs and the county associations for a greater allocation. Once the semi-final results were known, applications for tickets were being made. And with Manchester United having beaten Derby County there were going to be no spares from that quarter either. With six weeks to the Final, Blackpool were delaying the allocation of the tickets, but one thing was already being made clear: fans from the town and the Fylde coast would receive priority.

As befits a town with a reputation as a leading tourist attraction, the Wembley Final was quickly being viewed as a valuable marketing opportunity for Blackpool. One suggestion was for hats decked out in the football club's colours to be distributed with the words 'Blackpool is a holiday winner' emblazoned across them. A prototype sat on the desk of Alderman Jacob Parkinson when the council's publicity committee met. Then, as now, the town was not backward in pushing the name of Blackpool forward. Such an approach has helped ensure that the seaside resort is still a major tourist destination, just as it was in the 1940s.

When the tickets came to be distributed, it was inevitable there would be disappointment. Shareholders each received a ticket, as did each of the club's 5,000 season ticket holders. The supporters' club got an allocation, but as the membership had risen from 1,000 to 1,700 since the semi-final, not all were going to be successful. As the club pointed out, the allocation for Wembley with a 100,000 capacity was half what had been received for the semi-final at Villa Park, even though the ground held 30,000 less. The perennial problem of the social occasion of Wembley meaning that people received tickets at the expense of genuine fans would again raise its head.

With demand far outstripping supply, it was manna from heaven for the ticket touts who were offering to buy 3s (15p) Wembley tickets off season ticket holders as they collected them, for £3 each. There were reports of the black market price for four stand tickets being £50, a small fortune when the average weekly wage was around £6. Such was the interest, the precious cargo of tickets was held at the local police station in a strongroom before being brought under escort to the ground. Desperate fans swelled the queue to around 1,000, even though only season ticket holders were being sold the precious tickets. Cup fever had gripped Blackpool.

In the week before the Final, the Blackpool players travelled to nearby Lytham to practise on the grassy promenade that was reckoned to be the nearest thing to the lush Wembley turf. For all but the three internationals, Matthews, Mortensen and Johnston, it would be the players' first visit to Wembley. In the days before the Final the team stayed at an hotel in Ascot and used the facilities at Royal Wentworth Golf Club for training.

An injury worry concerned full-back Ronnie Suart, who twisted an ankle against Sunderland in a League match. He faced a desperate race to regain fitness, a battle he would lose in a trial at Wentworth Golf Course on the eve of the game. He went into a tackle with Jim McIntosh and was forced to admit he had lost the battle. It meant that John Crosland would have the chance of Wembley glory. Crosland was not a full-time professional, combining training twice a week with his articles as a chartered accountant. He would also be playing out of position. He was usually a centre-half, but would now be at left-back. The other full-back, Eddie Shimwell, fared better and successfully came through fitness tests to guarantee his place in the starting line-up. Manager Joe Smith had the difficult task of deciding which forward wouldn't be included. McIntosh had played in every Cup-tie en route to Wembley but was now to miss out. A paucity of goals since the semi-final, when he failed to hit the net in six League outings, proved his undoing. Alec Munro was given the nod for the inside-right spot. Shimwell spent the week practising penalty-kicks. It would be time well spent.

To try to cut down on pre-match nerves, the Blackpool team planned to arrive as near to the kick-off as possible. The teams were expected to be there at least an hour before, but the Seasiders were determined to be at the stadium certainly no sooner than that. The view of Stan Mortensen was that the team that settled first and forgot it was Wembley, but just another football match, would win the game.

Hugh Kelly recalls: "The first time going to Wembley is always the greatest. It is the best moment in a player's life. The whole build-up is something you never forget. We stayed at a beautiful hotel and were well looked after the whole time. I can remember travelling to Wembley with the police escort and our supporters cheering us as we approached the stadium. When we first got to the dressing-room I just walked around the place looking at it and trying to let it sink in that I was there. Then there was the walk up out of the tunnel. It was wonderful. The bee's knees. A truly great moment."

Ray Hall had not made the journey because he was recovering from tonsillitis. So while his father and brother set off for Wembley, he had to make do with listening to the match on the radio. He remembers the elation of the early goal and then things going from bad to worse, and at the end he was heartbroken. The praise being heaped on both teams for the football produced was of no consolation to the youngster.

Peter Collins had been lucky. Someone he knew had acquired a ticket and then at the 11th hour was unable to go and he was the beneficiary. He travelled down on the train and soaked up the atmosphere. He says: "Perhaps surprisingly I don't think I was ever worried about us winning or losing. The fact that we had got to Wembley and I was travelling to the big city to watch the Final was enough for me. Such was my faith in Blackpool at that time and the view I had that we were the top team, there was an attitude that if we didn't win it this time there would soon be another chance. It proved to be such a good game of football and really exciting that, although we lost, I thoroughly enjoyed the day."

Fans made the journey on 30 special trains and touts were asking 40 times the face value for tickets. It was estimated that not since the famous first FA Cup Final at Wembley in 1923, when Bolton Wanderers beat West Ham United 2-0 and a white police horse earned immortality for its role in helping to control a crowd of nearly a quarter of a million, had more supporters without tickets made the journey. One man was said to have offered a free week's holiday in Blackpool in return for a ticket. With Manchester United the opposition, all the fans were heading south and the Lancashire dialect could be heard everywhere. Fans of the Seasiders, wearing tangerine and white hats and huge rosettes, sat on the lions beneath Nelson's Column and tried to create more noise with their rattles than the Manchester supporters who had taken up station beneath Admiralty Arch with chants and cheers for their side. In the spirit of the age, that was the good natured way in which rivalry was expressed.

Once the teams had been presented to the King and Queen, two of the most skilful sides in English football, both with a reputation for playing attractive football, prepared to do battle. The game itself lived up to all expectations and even today is still talked of as one of the greatest Finals. Sadly for the Blackpool fans, the trophy would not be coming back with them. The final score of 4-2 to Manchester United flattered the winners, but there could be few complaints about the result against a side that just had the edge.

With the clash in colours, both sides wore a change strip. Blackpool took to the field in white while United were in blue. With two minutes gone, Matthews fashioned an excellent chance for Munro, who miss-hit the shot from close range. In the 14th minute, though, it was the Seasiders who took the lead. Mortensen was brought down on the edge of the penalty box and the referee pointed to the spot. It was a controversial decision with United players and fans claiming the foul was outside the penalty area. Undeterred, Shimwell showed that the practice he put in during the week before the match was not wasted and duly converted the kick.

Perhaps spurred by a sense of injustice, United came storming back. The pressure brought its reward when in the 30th-minute goalkeeper Robinson and Hayward dallied when a Delaney cross came over and Jack Rowley took advantage of the momentary lapse to equalise. Seven minutes later, Morty had achieved the rare feat of scoring in every round of the FA Cup when he got on the end of a Matthews free-kick. Blackpool still had the lead at half-time.

In the second period, Blackpool were far from overawed and Matthews was creating chances although the Manchester defenders were coping well with his crosses. Hopes that the lead could be increased were dashed when Hugh Kelly was penalised for handball. A quick free-kick by Johnny Morris saw Rowley again capitalise on a mix up between Robinson and Hayward. With ten minutes remaining, United were having the better of it, but Blackpool still had their chances. Now John Anderson made a long pass to Stan Pearson whose 25-yard shot beat Robinson. Minutes later the Cup was secure for Manchester when another shot by Pearson found the net. All agreed, it had been a marvellous game of football.

Syd Bevers, watching with the Atomic Boys, believes the turning point was the free-kick wrongly awarded against Hugh Kelly. "They scored from the free-kick and we never regained the initiative. It was a good game of football and the build-up to the game was superb. We made sure everybody knew we were there and helped create a good atmosphere. Although we had lost, everybody enjoyed the day out."

Kelly recalls: "It was a great game with open football. We were beaten, but up until halfway through the second half everybody was enjoying it and we were still in with a chance. They were worthy winners in the end. At the time we didn't realise what a good game it was, but later the fans were talking about it being one of the best matches seen. Certainly both teams walked off knowing they had played their best and I thought I had a good game. When I used to see supporters in the town later, I told them we had all played well and done our best."

Even after all these years he is still surprised at the decision to sell regular first-team goalkeeper Jock Wallace to Derby County. After the Final there was criticism of Robinson although Kelly would never countenance one player being singled out for blame. "Joe Robinson had to step in and he hadn't played much for the first team before. In the inquests afterwards, that was one of the points constantly being made. Blackpool had shown they were as good a team as any and on the day the two sides were well matched. Even though we lost, I felt good afterwards. We had been treated to the best food and hotels and it was a whole experience that I will never forget. I don't remember any tears at all among our players. We were disappointed, of course, but that was all."

The player said his thoughts also went back to the death of the club's owner, Colonel William Parkinson, after a match against Sheffield United. He remembers: "He had told the manager, Joe Smith, that his biggest ambition was to sit beside the King at Wembley and see us in the Final. As an incentive he stated if we did get to Wembley and win, he would put every married member of the side into a new house. I remember as the only single player in the team, asking about me. After the Sheffield game he stayed behind chatting to some of their directors and there was an argument. He collapsed and died. It was a tragedy that a man of his stature should miss out on seeing his ambition fulfilled so soon after."

In the aftermath of the Final, Joe Smith said that he thought that with 20 minutes to go and the team still winning, the Cup was theirs, but he knew the fortunes of football could change quickly and so it proved. He was proud of his players and the performance they had put in and also the way they had been magnanimous in defeat. At the dinner at the Mayfair Hotel in London that night, the view echoed time and again was that it was a match that would be remembered by all who saw it. Skipper Harry Johnston said the team had done their best and Manchester United had deserved their win. Matt Busby, the Manchester United manager, admitted: "We'd nearly given it up when you were still in front with only 20 minutes to go."

The most prophetic comment by a speaker at the dinner, though, was by A. V. Alexander, a Government minister and a director of Chelsea FC, when, as the *Evening Gazette* reported, he told the Blackpool team: "Take heart. You have been playing football in Blackpool for 50 years and only today came to Wembley. But it will not be another 50 years – not with a team such as you have built – before you are at Wembley again." It would, in fact, be only three years before they returned.

The Late 1940s

AWAY from the euphoria of the Cup Final, the closing seasons of the 1940s were a disappointment with the side never reaching the heights of their fifth place in the first season of League football after the war. There were, though, some sterling performances and some glorious football on display as Blackpool's side matured into an outfit capable of beating anybody on their day.

The distractions of the Cup in 1947-48 meant the team could perhaps be forgiven for letting their League performances slip towards the end of the season. After their semi-final win against Tottenham Hotspur on March 13, their League form slumped. In ten games the Seasiders could manage only two wins. There was a 3-0 win at Bloomfield Road against Arsenal, and Middlesbrough were beaten 1-0, also at home. Yet two of the most satisfying wins came after the Cup was lost.

Four days after the Final, the visitors to Bloomfield Road were Manchester United and it was a chance of revenge, even though it was of only small consolation. The newly-victorious Cup winners were outplayed and a 1-0 win did not do justice to Blackpool's superiority. The goalscorer was Mortensen and more than 32,000 were in the ground to see the performance. Indeed, beforehand there were queues a hundred yards long to get tickets for the match that was dubbed 'the Cup Final in miniature'.

Even though victory over Manchester United was sweet, there was an even better consolation prize three days later. Blackpool finished ninth in the League, but this last game was the highlight of the League programme. There is great rivalry among all the Lancashire clubs, but each have their own particular foe. For Blackpool, nearby Preston North End excite the strongest passions. Partisan fervour was heightened by the sub-text that accompanied the games at this time and through the 1950s. The Seasiders had Stanley Matthews, while at Deepdale there was the great Tom Finney. Who was the better was the source of great debate. Not surprisingly, the supporters of each side favoured their man. Now for the last match of the season, the Blackpool team and a small army of supporters made the journey to Preston. It was to be a match that would ruin summer holidays on the Golden Mile for the local supporters.

Many who were there professed they had never seen a game like it. The Blackpool supporters were pinching themselves that it was not a dream. Blackpool scored seven goals without reply as North End were played off the park. Jimmy McIntosh scored five to end his goalscoring drought and raise questions whether his omission from the Cup Final team might have been a mistake. The first came in the 25th minute when the reserve Preston goalkeeper watched seemingly spellbound as the ball bounced up in front of him and McIntosh applied the scoring header. The visitors' football was simple, direct and stunningly effective. The Seasiders even had Albert Hobson limping with a pulled muscle for three-quarters of the match, but the other four forwards coped admirably. What made the score even more remarkable was that both Stanley Matthews and Stan Mortensen were missing, although so too was Tom Finney. All three were on international duty with England.

After the first 20 minutes there was little for the visiting defenders to do except sit back and enjoy the show. McIntosh equalled the record of Jimmy Hampson as the highest individual scorer for Blackpool in a League match up to that time. Hampson scored five against Reading in November 1928. It was illustrious company for the Scot to keep. Fans of a certain age could still recall the exploits of Hampson, who was as famous in his heyday in the 1920s and 1930s as Matthews and Mortensen would be in later years. He still holds the club's goalscoring record with 252 in a 373-match career. He joined Blackpool in October 1927 from Nelson, for the not inconsiderable fee at the time of £1,000. He scored five goals in three games for England with the legendary Dixie Dean limiting his appearances in the international side. His end was tragic. He drowned in a boating accident in January 1938, at the age of 32. The town was shocked and even while Stan Matthews was performing his miracles on the wing there were many older supporters who still regarded the inside-forward as Blackpool's greatest player.

McIntosh had also secured another record that even the great Hampson could not match. It was a feat that Blackpool supporters would drop into friendly banter in years to come when they met the opposing fans in the days when conversations were still possible with sporting rivals and before tribal loyalties had brought segregation and destroyed much of the camaraderie that helped make going to football matches at this time special. It was that in Preston's 60 years in the Football League, it was the first time a player had put five past them. As the fans celebrated, their thoughts turned to the new season and hopes they could emulate the most successful campaign in their history.

Peter Collins had not been at Wembley but had the consolation of making the journey to Preston for the end of season jamboree at the North Enders' expense. "Lancashire sides were among the leading clubs in the division which seems unthinkable now. Preston were a good side and to go and put seven goals past them was unbelievable. The game against North End was one of the top games of the season. We didn't have the same rivalry with the other Lancashire clubs like Bolton, but with Preston it was always the one we wanted to win. I'm sure the Preston players and fans felt the same way. It was the local derby."

He remembers going in a crowd on the Ribble Bus from Blackpool to Preston. Others went on bikes and left them in the gardens of people living near the ground who they would look after them until they returned. The massive increase in car ownership has meant that many clubs have had to move to out-of-town stadiums in modern times, but owning a car was a rarity in the 1940s and the need for parking was largely non-existent. Collins remembers that McIntosh proving the goalscoring hero reinforced the views of many fans that he should have played in the Final. After such a rousing performance, it was hard to argue with his advocates on the way home.

The new campaign was to bring disappointment with a bottom-half-of-the-table, 16th place finish and no glory in the Cup. The euphoria of the previous season's historic victory over Preston was soon consigned to memory. After disposing of Second Division Barnsley, 1-0, the hopes of returning to Wembley to avenge the previous season's defeat at the Twin Towers did not survive the fourth round. After travelling to Stoke City, their former star Matthews helped his new side to a 1-1 draw and the replay at Bloomfield Road should have seen the side progress, but a 1-0 home defeat was a disappointment to players and fans alike.

Eleven wins in the season was not the form of a side hoping to challenge for the title, or even entertain hopes of being with the leading contenders. The previous season there was a worrying slump in form towards the close of the campaign, but that could have been attributed to players having half an eye on the Wembley Final. There was no such excuse this time, yet the team managed only one win in ten games. This did, though, coincide with a lengthy absence through injury of Matthews and Mortensen. It could be said that no team could hope to compete with the loss of two such key individuals. The season's biggest defeat came with a 5-0 reverse at Everton on March 5. The poor run of form was reflected in the attendances, which were generally down. The lowest was the 17,086 who saw Blackpool suffer a 3-0 defeat at home to Sheffield United. In a campaign of few highlights, the trip to Villa Park on New Year's Day was as good as it got.

There was also an evolution in the team's personnel with the departure of players who had been key figures as the club established itself after the war. They included Jimmy McIntosh, who joined Everton and was so unlucky to miss out on that Wembley appearance in 1948, although those on the terraces would not forget his five-goal haul against Preston North End in a hurry.

McIntosh had played alongside Harry Johnston at non-League Droylsden before beginning their Blackpool careers, and he would be given the chance of trying to replace Hampson after his death, although he was never able to make the inside-forward position his own. Although he made his first-team debut in September

1935, he could not command a regular place and went to Preston North End as part of a transfer deal that brought Frank O'Donnell to Bloomfield Road. After the war he was back at Blackpool, but only for three seasons.

Two key signings would play a significant role for Blackpool in the coming years. The first was Ewan Fenton, a dependable right-half who would be with the club for over 13 seasons. Fenton was from Dundee and was spotted playing for local Jeanfield Swifts before signing for Blackpool in November 1946. Harry Johnston ensured there were few first-team opportunities in his early days and although he made his first appearance in a draw with Derby County in September 1948, it was the 1952-53 season when he made a first-team spot his own. He played in that year's Cup Final and later in his career his calm authority saw him made captain. He left in May 1959 to play for Wrexham and also played for Limerick in the 1960-61 European Cup.

The second was a player synonymous with the great Blackpool side of the 1950s. While the brilliant forward line were banging them in up front, the towering presence of George Farm in the Blackpool goal was making life difficult for opposing forwards. He had been playing third-team football for Hibernian when he was signed for £2,700 in September 1948. A dedicated player, Farm worked hard on improving his game and made himself an automatic first-choice in the side. Thereafter, chances for reserve goalkeepers at Bloomfield Road were scarce. In his 12 seasons for the club he played in more than 500 games. He was capped ten times for Scotland and was 36 when he moved back north of the border to Queen of the South for £3,000.

For the trip to Villa Park in the League, Mortensen and Matthews were both available and were to feature on the score sheet. It was sometimes a criticism of Matthews that although he created plenty of goals, he did not score as many as his talents should have produced. However, his advocates stress that he created an awful lot for others. Certainly he was a handful for the Villa defenders in a 5-2 victory that was Blackpool's biggest of the season. An accurate long pass and some equally accurate shooting, both of which had been conspicuous by their absence for most of the season, were the tools with which the victory was forged. The goals were spread evenly with Munro, Kelly and Rickett also getting in on the act. There needed to be a few more results like this to lift supporters' spirits.

The late 1940s saw the emergence of what can only be described as a sporting phenomenon of the day. A group of fans dubbed themselves 'the Atomic Boys' and became a sporting institution, appearing at football grounds around the country and becoming almost as famous as Matthews himself. It was fitting that a town whose prosperity was built on its status as an entertainment capital should have a group of supporters steeped in showbiz tradition. They achieved quasi-official status at the club and their antics generated interest and newspaper headlines wherever they travelled.

Syd Bevers is one of the few surviving Atomic Boys and was a prime mover in their creation. He recalls: "The idea for the Atomic Boys came about when I ran a trip to Elland Road for a Leeds United game. It was during that match that I noticed Blackpool had very little colour among their fans. I chatted to a group of regular supporters I knew, and many were keen on putting that right. The original dress was tangerine coat, white trousers and a straw hat and we got really noticed at the 1948 Final. Then people started playing instruments; we had hand-bells and bugles. After that the whole thing took off."

Indeed, there were soon variations on the costumes. Bevers wore an oriental flowing robe in tangerine with a turban, one man dressed as a wartime WRVS complete with skirt and heels, a visit to Madame Tussauds in the town produced an array of uniforms including an 'Adolf Hitler' and 'Hermann Goering'. There was also a clown and a stilt walker. As well as the matches there were invitations to various fund-raising functions in the town. The main effort of the 15-strong troupe, though, was directed towards supporting Blackpool FC.

Bevers added: "We would go on the pitch before the match with the majority in tangerine and white suits and the rest dressed as well-known personalities or characters. A boy who worked on the Pleasure Beach suggested we should have a duck and brought one along. The duck became famous. He was first called Donald and then after England's humiliation by Hungary, he was named Puskas in honour of that great player. In fact, there were a number of different ducks through the years, but we always put one on the centre-circle before every game home and away. The duck achieved national fame."

He explained that getting the duck an orange colour proved a problem. "The first idea we had was to use a tangerine dye. We got the dye ready and put the duck in, and it came off like water off a duck's back, if you'll pardon the expression, so that was no use. Then a friend suggested using the colouring they use to stain Finnan haddock, which is a strong orange colour. I told the lad to hold the duck under the water for several minutes. Unfortunately he tried to do it in the house and the duck struggled, so the ceilings and walls were covered in orange when his mother came back. We now, though, had the orange duck. The Atomic Boys line-up was complete."

Eventually the numbers would grow and the organising and fund-raising became a major operation. Bevers reveals that as the Atomic Boys kept attempting to reach new heights with their gimmicks and stunts, there was a need to keep discipline. "Everybody enjoyed seeing us and that included the away fans as well as our own supporters. We had to keep our noses clean and make sure we didn't go too far. I had to do a lot of preaching to keep order. Drink could have taken a major part but I urged all of them to be careful. Anybody who put a foot wrong wouldn't be in next time. In truth, at one stage the whole thing got a little bit too big, but we had some great times."

Back on the playing front, the 1949-50 season certainly saw an improvement in form although Matthews was again too often missing. This time it was for a crucial 11-match spell in the second half of the season that again coincided with a depressing slump in form. An inability to maintain their high standards right to the end of the season ensured they finished no higher than seventh place, but it could have been much better. Whether the squad lacked the strength in depth of rivals at this time, or whether there was an over reliance on Matthews, the fans despaired when good League positions were allowed to slip as the campaign drew to a close. Certainly towards the end of this season it was rare for the exactly same team to take the field and this was at a time when successful teams rarely changed their line-up. The days of rotating players in a squad system were a long way off. A settled team was regarded as a prerequisite for success and with the maximum wage ensuring a much quieter transfer market, the first team could remain unchanged for years unless injuries took their toll.

Blackpool managed only one win in their last ten games and that was a 2-1 victory over Cup Finalists Arsenal at Bloomfield Road before a crowd of just over 32,000, which was close to capacity for the club. Given that the week before the players had performed before the biggest crowd of the season – 71,008 at Everton in a 3-0 defeat – it was proof that there was still huge support for football and that the Seasiders were a major draw wherever they played. Mortensen scored both goals against Arsenal towards what would be a League total of 22. There was, though, confusion over one. In a goalmouth mêlée three shots appeared to have been kept out by the Gunners, two cleared off the line and one hitting the post before South African Gordon Falconer volleyed it in for a goal on his debut. However, the referee ruled that an earlier shot by Mortensen had crossed the line before it was hacked clear.

Yet if goals were hard to come by at the close of the season – the last ten games saw only four scored – it had been a different story when Huddersfield Town were the visitors for the opening match on August 20. However, many fans put the 4-1 victory down as much to the failings of the Yorkshire side as to the talents of their own forwards. Yet there was an optimistic feeling that if Blackpool could repeat the performance, there would not be many teams who beat them.

In the Cup, hopes were briefly raised only to be dashed at the quarter-final stage. Wins over Southend United and Doncaster Rovers set up a fifth-round tie against a powerful Wolves side. Blackpool travelled to Molineux and a good defensive performance saw the game end goalless and set up a replay back at Bloomfield Road where a Mortensen strike proved enough to settle the tie.

However, a trip to Anfield proved an insurmountable obstacle with Liverpool progressing 2-1.

A player who made his mark towards the end of the season was to prove a key figure in the years to come. The South African Bill Perry was advised to join Blackpool by Billy Butler, manager of Perry's local team Johannesburg Rangers, after having turned down a move to Charlton Athletic the previous year. After making his League debut in March 1950, against Manchester United, he was to be a permanent fixture on the left wing during the club's most successful years. He won three caps for England and played 436 League and Cup games for Blackpool. During his career at Bloomfield Road, he scored 129 goals, but none was more famous than the winning strike in the 1953 Cup Final.

Still living in the town he remembers: "I was very fortunate to come to Blackpool at a very good time, when Matthews and Mortensen were here and we had a very good team. There was no professional football in South Africa, and Charlton recruited the biggest contingent of good players. Their manager used to come over in the English summer, which was our winter, looking for players and I was approached. Our trainer, Billy Butler, had played in the 1923 Bolton Wanderers Cup winning side with Joe Smith and he advised me not to rush into anything. He got in touch with Blackpool and recommended me. I was pleased I came to Blackpool because, not only was it a good club, it was also a nice place to stay."

Arriving at Bloomfield Road was something of a culture shock. "It was a big challenge. The standard was tremendously high compared with the amateur game in South Africa. For one thing the speed of the game as so much quicker. The weather was also a shock. It was very different. In Johannesburg they cancelled the match if it rained. I had to adapt to the changes and it does take time, yet I managed it quite quickly. Often I was playing on a pitch that was heavy. I had 11 games in the 'A' team and then the same number in the Reserves before I got promoted to the first team. It all happened within a season."

He recalls that first game away to Manchester United when the Seasiders won 2-1 thanks to two goals by Mortensen. "Even in those days, Manchester United had a good side and a big support. It was a huge attendance of more than 55,000 and I was understandably nervous. It suddenly sank in that I was in the first team playing on the opposite wing to Stanley Matthews and alongside all those great players. The captain, Harry Johnston, said to me as we were going out, not to be overawed and to play my own game. We got a win, which was a good start for me and I felt I had a good game. I got a good write-up in the newspapers and there was a lot of encouragement from the other players. Harry was the first to congratulate me at the end. Getting the first match under your belt helps a lot. I didn't look back after that and was a regular first-team player for ten years or so."

Also making his first appearance during the season was the amateur Bill Slater, or W. J. Slater, as he was titled at the time. His tenure at Bloomfield Road was brief, but he is likely to figure in sports pub quiz questions to tax aficionados of the club's history. He is the last amateur to appear in an FA Cup Final, having taken the field against Newcastle in 1951, and he holds the record for scoring Blackpool's fastest goal. It was against Stoke City in December 1949 and took only 11 seconds. He managed only 35 appearances in three seasons as he struggled to prise the number-ten shirt from Allan Brown. However, his career blossomed when, after a brief spell at Brentford, he joined Wolves. At Molineux he switched to half-back and now a semi-professional played 12 times for England as well as collecting three League championship medals and an FA Cup winners' medal. He was voted Footballer of the Year in 1960 and was awarded the OBE for his services to sport in 1982 in recognition not just of his distinguished playing career but also his work in physical education.

It is a measure of how far the Blackpool club had travelled in such a short space of time that a seventh place in the League and a Cup quarter-final could be regarded as a disappointment when not much more than a decade before it would have represented the best the club had achieved. The fans believed that the Seasiders could do better. The following season was to prove that such a belief was not ill-founded.

Sir Stanley Matthews

SIR Stanley Matthews was not only Blackpool's greatest player, but he can also lay claim to being England's finest footballer as well. It was not just the longevity of his career, which was in itself an amazing feat, but the way that he dominated both the domestic and world stage at a time when England were the world masters at the game. Nicknamed the Wizard of Dribble in Britain and known abroad as Der Zauberer (the magician), Matthews was the first ever European Footballer of the Year.

Certainly Jock Dodds, the centre-forward who played alongside him during wartime football for Blackpool and against him in England versus Scotland internationals, concurs with the foreign moniker. "As a player there was nobody better. He was at his peak when I played with him during the war and he was a magician. He could have joined the Magicians' Union if he had applied. For the poor full-back it was a case of now you see it now you don't when he had the ball. As a person he was a very nice man."

Another much-quoted accolade comes from the great Ferenc Puskas when, with both players long retired, the Hungarian had written a book and asked Matthews to help promote it in the UK. As Puskas was taking part in a photo call for the assembled media, he saw the England man standing on the touchline and raced across to greet him. Matthews said: "Puskas, you were the greatest." And Puskas said: "Maybe, but you are the very, very, all-time greatest."

Matthews' career stretched from well before World War Two to the 1960s. He was playing League football at 50. In 1951 he feared his international career was drawing to a close and that perhaps there was a feeling in the corridors of power that he was too old. Yet six years later he was still gracing the international stage, making the last of his 54 appearances against Ireland in 1957. If his first two England games, as a 19-year-old against Wales and Italy in 1934, had not gone well, he quickly made amends and although he would too often fall foul of selectors, he rarely failed the side on the field.

Certainly he had his critics. There were those who questioned his work-rate, his lack of heading or tackling ability and the fact that he scored few goals. Yet as the Blackpool centre-forward Ray Charnley, who played alongside him, says: "He may not have scored many goals but Stan made a hell of a lot. He was a great player who could take on and beat a man and that is very rare in the modern game."

Nat Lofthouse, the Bolton Wanderers and England centre-forward, recalls how having Matthews on one wing and Tom Finney on the other made his job with England so much easier. "They were both great players. With those two I didn't have to be good with my feet. All I had to do was wait for those two to get the crosses over, lace facing away, and I would have a chance of getting to it with my head. We will never see another like Stanley Matthews. He was the great player."

The war had severely curtailed both his international and domestic career and after the hostilities ended he found himself overlooked for most of the 1946-47 season in favour of Tom Finney, the Preston North End outside-right and his only serious rival for the title of outstanding player of his generation. After Matthews made his post-war debut, against Switzerland, an injury to Bobby Langton provided the ideal solution to England's dilemma. Finney switched to outside-left and both the stars of the day could be accommodated. For the international against Portugal in Lisbon the mouth-watering England forward line-up consisted of Finney, Tommy Lawton, Stan Mortensen, Wilf Mannion and Matthews. A 10-0 rout was the outcome.

The fans of their respective clubs long argued the merits of who was the better player, yet such debates never troubled the two football legends. Off the field Finney and Matthews were friends. Finney tells how they used to travel together to England training sessions and international matches and would discuss football in general and swop notes on full-backs they had played against, sharing tips on strengths and weaknesses of the players whose life on the field they could make a misery.

In his early days there had been some suggestions voiced in certain sections of the media that Matthews did not have a big-match temperament. His career gave the lie to that and so do the players who starred alongside him. Finney recalls: "There was nothing Stan liked more than playing on the big stages. That was the mark of him and so many other great players. Give them the big night, the big opponents and the big atmosphere, and they will rise to it. He always seemed to bring his best football to the biggest games."

Matthews played in the days when the winger had just one job to do. Beat his man and fire over cross after cross and that was what he did. Nine times out of ten he would opt to go down the touchline. Finney regards him as having the best close control of any player he has seen and a terrific turn of pace. There was also the famous swerve that left opponents momentarily off balance. He has no doubt that although the winger's role in the modern game may have changed, there would still be a place for a player with the skills of Matthews.

Two games stick out in Finney's mind as great examples of Matthews at his peak. Perhaps some will be surprised that his selection does not include the 1953 Cup Final when he helped conjure victory from certain defeat. Rather the games were on the international stage and although Finney is too modest to mention it, he was no mean performer in both games as well. How blessed England were in those days. The first was at Wembley in December 1954, against a West Germany team that had just won the World Cup. England won 3-1, playing some wonderful football, and Matthews was in inspirational form. The second was the last time the two played together, in May 1957 against Denmark in Copenhagen and England won 4-1. Incredibly, Matthews was 42 then and still taking centre stage.

Matthews was born at Hanley in the Potteries, the son of a boxer, Jack Matthews, 'the fighting Barber of Hanley'. Jack encouraged all his children to keep fit and introduced them to deep-breathing exercises that were to play an important part in Stan's keep-fit regime throughout his life. Fellow players at Blackpool recall that Matthews had his own training schedule that involved not only deep breathing but also runs on the beach at the seaside resort. In fact he was decades ahead of his time in his diet and training programme. It was more akin to the demands on modern footballers rather than the few-laps-round-the-pitch workouts that constituted training for the majority of players in his day.

Hugh Kelly recalls: "Stan had his own way of keeping fit. He was getting on in years when he came to Blackpool and used his own methods. They kept him at the top long after his contemporaries had retired. He would be up at 6am, running while the rest of us were still in bed. He was a great believer in deep breathing. He never preached but if you were interested in his methods he would explain them. I took his example with deep breathing and still do it to this day. It's a great asset to a sportsman. The air in Blackpool is marvellous. Nobody took any notice that Stan didn't work out with us, but did his own thing. He had an agreement with the club and he was so respected. He also played a lot of tennis on his own court at home."

He rejects the idea that Matthews wouldn't last five minutes in the modern game with defenders willing to resort to illegal means to slow him down. In his playing days there were full-backs who would try to use foul means to stop him, but they rarely succeeded. Matthews was too quick and could make them look fools. He also never retaliated when he was fouled. He would just get up and carry on. Peter Collins remembers seeing a defender lunge at Matthews, intent on taking man and ball and connecting with only fresh air. He ended up on his backside with the laughter of the crowd ringing around his ears.

The player also endeared himself to the sporting public and his fellow professionals with his manner off the field. He was a reflective man who was never big-headed about his triumphs or his skills. He was quiet and in some ways shy. He tended to avoid the spotlight. On the field there was no petulance, no arguing with referees, no trying to get a fellow professional sent-off with play acting. His feet did all the talking and he was content with that.

One anecdote highlighting how he shunned the limelight concerns a night out in London's West End on the eve of a Cup-tie against Fulham in 1948, a Cup run that would end at Wembley. The players, along with wives and girlfriends, were at the Victoria Palace where the Crazy Gang were starring. All evening the Gang were calling out for Stan every few minutes and one of them paraded up and down the aisles paging him. Yet not only did he resist all entreaties to make himself known, the player sank lower and lower in his seat in an attempt to make himself invisible.

Allan Brown remembers: "Stan was a very modest man for the undoubted star that he was. It showed in the way he always credited Morty with the man-of-the-match in the 1953 Final. Yet there isn't a player in football today who has his talent. Nobody can take on a player and beat him the way he did. Matthews would have been a great player if he was performing today in the same way he was during our own era. He had everything." And these were the days when a pass back brought a chorus of jeers from your own fans. Modern players would be deaf with the catcalls. What the paying public wanted was to see all-out attacking football.

Dodds recalls that although the maximum wage meant that the most Matthews earned during his playing days with Blackpool was £20 a week, the player was sharp when it came to earning money from outside the game. Of course, it was nothing compared to what modern players can earn. But he was paid for testimonial appearances, writing newspaper columns and such like. His mind could also be as quick as his feet at times.

He recalls that during the height of the terrorist troubles in Ireland, Matthews and Jackie Mudie were invited to Dublin for a personal appearance at a function. The two often appeared together as Stan tried to get his old centre-forward partner involved as an after-dinner speaker to earn him a few quid. When they arrived in the Irish capital there was a suite for Stan with flowers and a card welcoming him. Jackie had an ordinary single room. Yet Matthews was adamant that his friend should have the better room and while he at first declined, eventually Jackie accepted the gracious gesture. At breakfast the next morning Mudie told Stan he'd had a good night and asked why he had let him have the suite. "I don't trust those IRA buggers," was the legend's reply. He was not going to be an easy, high-profile target for the terrorists.

Walter Horan was a well-known comedian on the northern club circuit and a frequent entertainer at sportsmen's dinners, where he was known by his stage name of 'Wandering Walter'. He recalls that Matthews was sometimes the guest speaker and they would share a car home. "I remember when he first brought me back from a do, he was so ordinary, so down to earth. I mean that in a nice way. There was nothing of the prima donna about him. He was quite a shy person and he needed bringing out of his shell. As an after-dinner speaker he didn't have to tell jokes, his presence was enough. People just listened to what he had to say because he had achieved so much."

Although Matthews supplemented his income with extra work, he never envied the wealth of the modern footballer. What he did object to was the deterioration in standards on the field. The feigning and petulance of modern players. The way the tough but basically honest nature of the game in his era had given way to the dissent and deceit of the modern game. Not long before his death he said: "I'll tell you how different it was when I started. Before the war, if you got sent-off you were booed by your own fans. And if you were sent-off playing for England you never played for your country again."

Matthews was an outstanding schoolboy footballer and once scored a dozen goals in a game playing at centre-half. He played for England Schoolboys before being taken on by his local club, Stoke City, straight from school at the age of 14 in 1929. He worked in the office for a while until he turned full-time professional. His League debut came at the age of 17. However, both just before and after the war, he had difficult relations with the manager, Bob McGrory, and with the resumption of League football in 1946-47 he found himself on the sidelines.

It provided a golden opportunity for Blackpool to sign the

talented winger. Matthews had played for the club during the war and opened a small hotel in the town. If he served his apprenticeship at Stoke, and would perform his swansong at the Potteries club, then his glory years would be in the tangerine shirt of Blackpool. He was signed for the princely sum of £11,500 and the fortunes of both club and player were set to soar.

Matthews' first game for Blackpool was while he was serving in the RAF during World War Two and was stationed in the town. He was invited by Colonel William Parkinson to guest for the team and his first game was against the great rivals, Preston North End in August 1941. That ended in defeat, but he helped establish the Seasiders as a major force in football during the war years and took part in the 1943 War Cup challenge match against Arsenal at Stamford Bridge when he played a major part in an impressive 4-2 victory, described by some eye-witness accounts as the best performance ever by a Blackpool side.

Matthews was 32 when he signed for Blackpool on May 10, 1947, and yet again the detractors were saying the best years were behind him. He was to confound them with his performances at both club and international level in the coming years, appearing in all three of Blackpool's FA Cup Finals of the late 1940s and early 1950s. Certainly among the Stoke faithful there were no doubts as to his prowess with thousands turning up to protest meetings in an attempt to overturn the decision by City to sell him.

In the 1957 New Year's honours list he was awarded the CBE and eight years later became the first soccer knight. He was Footballer of the Year in 1948 and 1963. For the latter he was back playing at Stoke City and was now aged 48. He had returned to Stoke in 1961 and two years later helped them regain their First Division status. He was awarded his knighthood in 1965 while still playing, although the year also marked his last match in League football, playing against Fulham at the age of 50 years and five days. In all he played 710 League games for Stoke and Blackpool. When the curtain finally came down on his playing career, he had a spell as manager of Port Vale after an acrimonious parting with Stoke City. By 1967, though, he decided management was not for him. He later went to live in

Malta, where he played for the Hibernians team at 55, and to coach widely abroad especially in South Africa and in Canada before returning to live in the Potteries.

The player himself had highs and lows in his career. And not just involving winning and losing matches. He regarded the low point as a sixth-round Cup-tie against Bolton Wanderers in March 1946 while he was still with Stoke City. A huge crowd was expected, boosted by the presence of Mathews himself, but the match is remembered not for his artistry on the wing but as one of the darkest chapters in the annals of the game. The official figure shows an attendance of 65,419, but probably more than 85,000 had been shoehorned into a Burnden Park ground not fully opened because part of it was being used to stockpile food still being rationed after the war. In the crush that ensued, 33 supporters were killed and another 500 were injured. It was to be Matthews' most tragic match.

In the Stoke dressing-room before the game, the players had been given their last instructions from manager Bob McGrory, who urged them to throw themselves into the tie from the off to try to overturn a two-goal deficit from the first leg. There was confidence in the ranks. That it was a huge crowd was obvious as they ran out, but it was expected for the Cup-tie. Supporters spilling out on to the side of the pitch to get a better view was also not unusual. What quickly became apparent, however, was this crowd was pouring on to the playing surface.

In his autobiography *The Stanley Matthews Story* he says: "Then I got the feeling that there was more in this sudden invasion than met the eye." It was only after the game had been halted and the players reached the sanctuary of the dressing-room that the news was relayed that there had been deaths on the terraces. About hearing the news that the game was to be completed Matthews wrote: "We got up and sadly walked down the tunnel on to the field once more. One angry spectator, who must have been told about the deaths, caught hold of Frank Baker, the outside-left, and shouted: 'Tis a crime to carry on.' This was silly talk, we were doing our job. As footballers we came under the orders of the referee; and if he said play, then play we did."

It was a source of great regret to the player that the lessons of Burnden were never really learnt and the fans continued to be packed into grounds that were largely Victorian. It would be 43 years later with the Hillsborough disaster before major changes were brought about in the way the game treated the people who filed through the turnstiles.

The great moments for Matthews were, of course, legion, both in the white shirt of England and the tangerine of Blackpool, yet he himself regards his finest hour as the FA Cup win in 1953 when he finally had the medal he promised his late father he would collect. It was a victory particularly sweet after the two defeats he suffered with Blackpool in 1948 and 1951. Now 38 years old, he knew this would probably be his last chance and the way that victory was snatched from the jaws of defeat makes the match one of the most remarkable in Wembley history. As befits the modest man he was, he found the whole 'Matthews Final' publicity embarrassing.

During his lifetime they erected a life-size bronze statue, showing him on the ball poised to dribble past a hapless defender. The inscription says: 'His name is symbolic of the beauty of the game, his fame tireless and international, his sportsmanship and modesty acclaimed.' Whether such a private and shy man appreciated having to walk past his own statute to go to the shops is hard to tell, although he was probably quietly proud of the tribute erected to the town's most famous son. Certainly those few words succinctly sum up the man.

His death on February 23, 2000, at the age of 85, was on the eve of an England game against Argentina before a packed Wembley stadium. His second wife, Mila, had died shortly before and he was said to be heartbroken at her loss. The players lined up for a minute's silence before the international. Millionaire celebrity footballers paid their respects to a player who had almost certainly hung up his boots before all but a couple were born and whose conduct on and off the field encapsulated a footballing era now passed. Yet for all their money, the sponsorship deals and the Hollywood film star lifestyles, will any of them capture the imagination in the way that the Wizard of Dribble so captivated audiences over four decades?

In Search of The Double

THE 1950-51 season was one where, for a time, the Holy Grail of the game, the Double, looked possible as Blackpool enjoyed a wonderful season that was sadly to see them fail at the final hurdles. They finished a creditable third in the League and their FA Cup exploits ensured another trip to Wembley. This time their opponents were Newcastle United and there was again heartbreak with a comprehensive 2-0 defeat. It seemed Stanley Matthews would never win the medal that he admitted had become an obsession for him.

Fellow players remember Matthews arriving from the summer break full of confidence and eager for the new season to get under way. There was a feeling in the camp that the side was reaching a peak and that they were capable of producing some very good performances. The legendary winger later admitted that he was thinking about a Wembley date and the chance to collect a winners' medal before a ball had been kicked. This was now a Blackpool side that feared nobody and with good reason.

Newly-promoted Tottenham Hotspur provided the opposition for the opening game of the season and for the match at White Hart Lane they were made clear favourites. However, all the Lancashire clubs at this time were used to London clubs being talked-up by the national press, who were based on their doorstep, while for the small-town clubs in the red rose county, recognition was harder to gain. It was said one good win in the capital was worth half a dozen at Bloomfield Road as regards the publicity it generated. Yet as one jaundiced scribe on the local *Evening Gazette* reflected: "London teams are not always as good as the London critics exultantly report them to be."

Spurs had won the Second Division championship by nine points and had praise heaped on them for the attractive style of their football. They were now about to discover that the gulf between the divisions can be a wide one as Blackpool handed out a football lesson, and a dose of harsh reality, as much to the press advocates of the team as to the club itself. The last time the sides met was in the semi-final of the Cup in 1948, when the Seasiders triumphed in extra-time. It would not be so close this time before a crowd of just under 65,000.

Stanley Matthews proved the outstanding individual, but it was nonetheless a superb team display that swept Spurs aside 4-1. Defying the critics who were starting to write off his football career – could those who believed his days were numbered have possibly foreseen the longevity in the game he would achieve? – the Wizard of Dribble was back at his tantalising best, beguiling defenders and carving chances for those around him. There were two goals for Harry Johnston and one each for Stan Mortensen and Hugh Kelly. To be fair to Spurs, they were a good side and played an attractive, close-passing game, but on the day Blackpool were better.

Such a stirring start to the season and such a memorable match whetted the appetites for the fare that was to follow. No win in the next four games, with Burnley taking three points off the side, did not encourage too much optimism, but as the season progressed, glimpses of the form of that opening match returned. A 1-1 draw against Manchester United on December 30 was the start of a 13-match unbeaten run that forced Blackpool into contention for the title. Mortensen again demonstrated his talents, hitting the net 15 times in this period.

Earlier in the month, in a 3-2 win against Charlton Athletic, another Bloomfield Road legend made his first appearance. Allan Brown had been signed from East Fife for £26,500 and, with Mortensen, the inside-forward would play a major part in

Blackpool's pre-eminence in the 1950s, before his departure in December 1957 to Luton Town for close to £10,000. He would appear on the losing side in the 1959 Cup Final against Nottingham Forest, but was fated never to wear the tangerine shirt at Wembley. He played for Scotland in the 1954 World Cup finals.

He recalls: "There were already a few Scots at Blackpool and I knew Jackie Mudie and George Farm. I didn't really know how good a team Blackpool were, but I certainly knew Stanley Matthews. As a boy I had bought a book about his life and what he went through as part of his fitness and training and I used to copy it. I also used to compete in running events at Highland Games. Little did I think then that I would be playing alongside the man himself. When I heard there was interest in me, I was happy. I was fit and willing to go anywhere providing it benefited my playing career. East Fife gave me a benefit out of the transfer fee. I arrived in Blackpool as the club were having a great season."

The successful League run ended with a 2-1 defeat away to Huddersfield Town. It was not just the defeat that brings back unhappy memories for Brown. He jumped for the ball and twisted his knee. The medical diagnosis was not promising. The cartilage damage meant his season was over. He played in every round of the Cup but now missed the Final. "It was disappointing, but just one of those things in football. You can't pull out of tackles or not go for the ball because of worries about injuries."

The following week, on April 14, Middlesbrough were the visitors against a Blackpool side with eight players missing through injury or international call-ups. Both sides were hoping for at least a top-four place. With Matthews and Mortensen missing, the side did well to come through with a 2-1 win that was testament to hard work and a determination to grind out a win. It also showed the all-round strength of the side. This was no longer a team too dependent on one or two stars. Jackie Mudie and Willie McIntosh collected the goals.

Mudie had joined the club as an amateur from junior side, Lochee Harp, in his native Dundee and signed professional forms in June 1947. He had the best possible start, scoring the only goal on his debut in a win over Liverpool at Anfield in March 1950.

Watching on the sidelines was Bill Perry and he remembers Mudie played very well and looked like being a regular in the first team in the years to come.

As Blackpool challenged for League and Cup glory the following season, Mudie was a regular in the side, only to lose his place with the arrival of Ernie Taylor the following year. By 1953 he was back and played in the Cup Final and with the departure of Mortensen in 1955, he switched from inside-forward to centre-forward, although at 5ft 6ins he was small for the position. Yet he still proved an accomplished goalscorer and beat far larger defenders in the air. He played in 356 games for Blackpool and scored 155 goals. The Scotland selectors were quick to take note and he played 17 times at international level, scoring nine goals, a total that included a hat-trick against Spain. In March 1961 he joined Stoke City and continued his partnership with Stanley Matthews.

Blackpool's League campaign ended disappointingly with defeats inflicted by Sheffield Wednesday and Arsenal in the final two matches of the season. Manchester United won the title and Spurs had recovered sufficiently from their opening match defeat at the hands of Blackpool to finish as runners-up. It had, though, been a successful year although to the delight of the fans the performance was overshadowed by the achievements in the Cup. The Seasiders were to find themselves back on the road to Wembley.

Five players who had tasted defeat against Manchester United in 1948 would return to try to rectify the wrong and lift the trophy on this occasion. Matthews, Mortensen and the captain Harry Johnston were joined by Eddie Shimwell and Eric Hayward. Yet again the spirits of the town would be lifted by the success of the local football team. Everywhere the talk was of the side's progress in the competition and whether they could return to the Twin Towers. And once a Final place was assured, whether they could this time triumph on the Wembley stage.

The draw for the third round presented Blackpool with First Division opposition at the first hurdle in the form of Charlton Athletic, although they were down in the relegation zone. On League form a visit to The Valley should have held little fear with the

Seasiders having lost only once in five visits since the war, but in the Cup anything can happen and it was a tough opening test. A fortnight before the January 6 date, Blackpool had visited Charlton and won 3-2 in the League. Whether through confidence or apathy, the Cup fixture had not caught the imagination of the seaside town's support with only an estimated 200 travelling down to London. The players to fear were reckoned to be the Charlton centre-forward Charlie Vaughan and the goalkeeper Sam Bartram.

Bartram certainly had his work cut out, yet a gallant performance by the Londoners nearly saw Blackpool as third-round casualties. Twice it was Charlton who took the lead and although the visitors had the class and created panic in the home defence, they failed to make the most of their opportunities. For an hour, Athletic were effectively reduced to ten men with an injury to inside-forward Tom Evans, yet it didn't deter them. Bill Perry equalised for the first time but with four minutes remaining Charlton had the lead and the place in the next round until Mortensen intervened to send the tie to a replay.

Brown remembers: "I'd not been playing First Division football long and the pace was faster than what I was used to. I was completely knackered at the end. I remember I was suffering from cramp and in a bit of a state, but I kept going. Although I didn't score, I had a good game and was settling into the side. It was a better standard than I was used to, but I felt I was coping. It was too early for anybody except the fans to start thinking of Wembley after the first game."

The winners of the replay faced a home tie against Third Division North Stockport County and an unchanged Blackpool side were determined to ensure it would be them after earning such a late reprieve. A 'flu epidemic had not taken its toll on the players, but had depleted the groundstaff and the pitch was expected to be a sea of mud. Rumours that Matthews would not be playing proved unfounded.

While the opening exchanges were evenly contested, as the first half wore on Blackpool began to have the better chances and in the 38th minute the opening goal fell to them when a Matthews corner was met by a diving Mortensen header. There were two more clear chances which first the centre-forward and then Perry failed to convert before, with a minute to go before half-time, Perry made a 50-yard dash down the line and hit a deep cross which Morty again successfully met with his head. A third, scored by Mudie, made the game safe.

A spying mission by Stockport at the game did not yield enough secrets to affect the result of the next round, with Blackpool progressing 2-1 with the Mortensen and Mudie combination again providing the goals. The Seasiders were first out of the bag again when the draw was made for the fifth round of the Cup and the visitors to Bloomfield Road were Mansfield Town, who would be that season's Third Division North runners-up. A comfortable 2-0 win saw Blackpool meet Fulham in the quarter-final and they also found a trip to the coast too much of a barrier to their Cup hopes, succumbing by the narrowest of margins with a Brown penalty the only score.

Blackpool were again in the semi-final and, as it had in 1948, fortune again smiled on them. They had faced Second Division opposition in the form of Spurs three years before, and it was from the same division their opponents were drawn this time. The Seasiders would meet Birmingham City (who had been relegated from the top flight the year before) at Maine Road, Manchester. The other semi-final was an all-First Division affair with Newcastle United playing Wolves at Hillsborough.

For Peter Collins, the semi-final was special because he got to travel to the game with the Atomic Boys. He was an apprentice at the Hawker aircraft company working alongside one of the regular Atomic Boys and was invited to travel with them. "It was incredible. A chance of a lifetime to be involved with them. They were as famous at the time as the players. Everybody was dressed up and there was the parade around the ground. Their theme tune was *Yes, We Have No Bananas* and the crowd sang it. It was all great fun even if the match proved a bit of a disappointment."

Birmingham could not be taken too lightly, having already accounted for Manchester United and then won a tough encounter at Derby County. The Blackpool players could also expect to be harried and hassled in a bid to knock them out of their stride. There would be some fierce tackles and a good few would be aimed at Matthews. However, the Blackpool fans were confident. Much was made in the pubs and cafés of the town of the excellent post-war record the side had against the Midlanders in the League. They had never been beaten and there was confidence, they would not be beaten on this occasion. Cup fever had taken hold and there was a rush for the tickets with a capacity 73,000 expected. Twenty thousand of those were from the seaside resort.

In a close-fought match there were no goals but as the fans headed for home, both sets of supporters could reflect on what might have been. Jacky Stewart, for Birmingham, had contrived to hit goalkeeper Farm's leg when the goal was at his mercy and then, with two minutes remaining, a fierce shot from the same player hit the post. On such moments are Cup-ties won and lost. Blackpool had their chances, although their cause was not helped by an injury to Mortensen that left him a second-half passenger. The centre-forward did, though, still manage a header which the goalkeeper Gil Merrick got finger-tips to and it was enough to see it hit the bar. Earlier, Bill Perry beat the full-back and his shot went past Merrick, only for it to be cleared off the line. At the end, many fans thought extra-time would be played but the referee led the teams from the field and it seemed even the players were taken by surprise. A public address announcement was needed to persuade reluctant fans that it was all over, for the day at least. The next stop was a replay at Goodison Park.

Four days later, and with Mortensen recovered from his arm injury, Blackpool made sure of their place in the FA Cup Final. The result was 2-1 but that score should have been more. That it wasn't was testament to a Birmingham side who, although they were outplayed, remained resolute in defence and in the closing minutes threw everything into a desperate attack that saw even Matthews back in defence clearing corner-kicks away. Mortensen had given his side the lead and it should have been greater as Blackpool enjoyed much of the attacking play but were unable to extend their advantage. Then with 65 minutes gone, the lead was extended courtesy of a glorious Perry goal when he raced 40 yards or more and shot. Yet City had the strength of character to fight back and they got a goal they deserved. Now for the closing minutes it was backs-to-the-wall stuff for the Seasiders as their 10,000 travelling supporters willed them to hold out. Shots were blocked, a header cleared from under the bar and wonderful saves made by Farm to ensure another day out at Wembley for the Lancashire side.

Perry remembers the game: "Birmingham had given us a tough battle and the tie went to a replay. I picked the ball up on the halfway line, ran up the wing and then cut inside. I looked up with the intention of crossing to Morty and, then at the last second, I changed my mind and, as the goalkeeper came out to cover the expected cross, I shot and it went in. The goalkeeper was caught on the wrong foot. It was one of those things that happens in a split second and this time it came off. We still had some work to do, they hit the post and George Farm pulled off a few good saves, but we were through. Stan Matthews always said that in many ways the semi is more important than the Final. If you go through you are there in front of 100,000 spectators and just appearing at Wembley is magic. If you lose the semi it's all over and you're forgotten. I agree with Stan on that. Although we lost the Final that year, it was a tremendous experience."

Hugh Kelly recalls: "A problem was that Birmingham were strangers to us. They were in the Second Division and we didn't really know much about them. When they held us to a draw it was a shock to us as much as to the fans. In the replay they took us all the way. Birmingham had played well. They had no players in their side of any great note, but they played as a team and we were very happy to get through without the need for extra-time."

After travelling three years before, only to be thwarted, the 12,000 fans who made the journey to Wembley were optimistic this would be their year. There had been the usual scramble for tickets, the complaints about the allocation and the desperate following up of rumours about where the precious slips of paper could be obtained. As they had in their build-up to the Manchester United Final, the players had been to Lytham promenade to make the most of the lush green sward that was similar to Wembley. On their departure from the town for the game, 2,000 people were at Central Station to cheer them off and fog detonators placed on the line exploded as the train set off on its journey. Morty had walked through the crowds wearing a disguise that fooled nobody – plastic nose, false teeth and moustache and a black Homburg hat.

Bill Perry remembers that the team stayed at an hotel in Harrow and tried to go about their training and keep the build-up to the match as low-key as possible, although the excitement was rising all the time. He was looking forward to the game and as far as he was concerned it couldn't come soon enough. The whole town was behind the players and after losing in 1948, before he arrived, he knew there was a feeling that this should be the year they brought the Cup back to the town.

The reports from the stadium itself were that the pitch would be in perfect condition for fast football. Wembley officials were also keen to discourage anyone from travelling to the ground without a ticket. The size of the operation for the Cup Final was highlighted when it was announced there would be 250 police officers, 500 FA stewards, 400 commissionaires and 500 other staff. A clampdown on ticket touts had been ordered with warnings of a £2 fine for anyone caught dealing in tickets on the roads approaching the ground. It did not prevent a thriving market with 3s (15p) tickets being sold for £2 and up to £10 for one guinea (£1.05) seats.

The catering needs of the crowd would involve 30,000 cups of tea, 15,000 bottles of soft drinks, 40,000 tubs of ice cream and, in the days when fans could be trusted to drink alcohol in the ground without starting a riot, 12,000 bottles of beer were ready to quench thirsts. Everything was ready for those lucky enough to get a ticket either through proper channels or from the black market.

The Atomic Boys were given a civic send off at the Town Hall before they began their journey south. A crowd of more than 1,000 was outside to see them go. The Mayor and Deputy Mayor had already departed for London, but councillors and council officers joined the Boys on the balcony to toast Blackpool's success in beer and there was even a glass for the mascot, Stanley the Duck, as the crowd cheered below. The banner across the side of the Atomic Boys coach read: 'Shimwell, Minister of Defence.' Syd Bevers remembers having a quick chat with Stan Matthews who asked him whether they would be trying to put the duck on at Wembley and to be careful lest they get thrown out for their trouble and miss the match.

Once in London, the Atomic Boys joined more than 4,000 Blackpool fans in Trafalgar Square. A lone policeman had the uphill task of trying to keep the orange-bedecked supporters away from the base of Nelson's Column. Certainly the Atoms were not to be kept at bay and they climbed the lions and went through their repertoire of antics to the amusement of the crowd. The site was an unofficial meeting point for the Blackpool fans, yet one Newcastle fan in his black and white colours also got on to the lion and was given a huge cheer by the Lancashire supporters. The only confrontations this day would be on the pitch. Everybody else was set to enjoy their day in London. From the early hours there had been cries of "Up the 'Pool," ringing around the centre of London as fans arrived by coach, train and car.

As the kick-off time approached, Bevers made his move. He said: "I smuggled the duck into the ground in a shopping bag with a zip top. I was helped because I had a seat near the front and all I had to do was climb over the barrier and nip on. I was a bit more agile in those days. The fans were expecting it because I had been in the papers beforehand saying the duck was going to be taken on. It was a tradition and I got away with it. When I reached the centre-circle I let it out. The fans liked to see the duck because it was supposed to bring us a bit of luck. We lost 2-0 so that didn't work but it was a good stunt. Wembley wouldn't officially let us on but I think because we had become so well-known and respected, they let me get away with it. When I got back to my seat, a couple of stewards came over and said putting a duck on the centre-circle wasn't allowed. I had to be very apologetic and promise I wouldn't do it again."

Perry can still vividly recall the final minutes before kick-off: "There were butterflies in my stomach leading up to the match. The size of the crowd and the noise was unbelievable. It was a wonderful experience before the kick-off and then, as soon as the whistle blew, the nerves were forgotten and I concentrated on the game. When it

was over and we had lost, that was when I learnt what a demor-
alising feeling it is to be on the losing side in a Cup Final. The
winning team are doing their lap of honour holding the Cup aloft
and we were standing there with our heads bowed, waiting for it to
end. It was a depressing experience. We ran towards the end where
our supporters were and got cheered, but I felt rotten. It was a lot
worse for players like Matthews, Morty and Johnston who had been
there in 1948. It was doubly sad for them and there was a sense that
their careers were moving on and this might be their last chance."

If the match three years before had been memorable for the
football displayed despite the result, then on this occasion Blackpool
did not even have that consolation. They were outplayed by a side
of whom, on paper, they should have at least been the equals if not
had a slight edge over. Fans would later rue a tactical decision by
manager Joe Smith to play an offside trap to nullify the great Jackie
Milburn and offer some protection to Eric Hayward, who it was
feared did not have the pace to cope with the Newcastle centre-
forward. The defenders were not comfortable with the ploy and it
was to prove the side's undoing.

Peter Collins recalls: "The Newcastle game was a bit of a damp
squib. I was much more upset losing that game than the United Final
in 1948. The day was dull, the game was dull and we played badly.
There wasn't the excitement or the quality of football there had been
with the United game. Then, of course, it was the first time
Blackpool had reached a Cup Final and that was an event in itself.
Now we felt the team deserved to win something and there was the
desire for Stan Matthews to get his medal. Our defending on the day
though was horrendous"

The better of the early exchanges were enjoyed by Blackpool and
both Slater and Mortensen had chances in the opening ten minutes.
Then Milburn began to get the better of the defence and the offside
trap was beaten four times early on with Farm and the post saving the
day. The Blackpool fans thought they were a goal down when Milburn
got the ball in the net, only for the offside trap to have done its job
and the goal was ruled out. Matthews was working hard, but finding
Bob Corbett in no mood to let him have his own way.

The game remained goalless at half-time but five minutes after the restart, George Robledo intercepted a pass from Matthews and put Milburn through. The defenders vainly relied on an offside decision being given, but this time there was no reprieve as the centre-forward's shot beat Farm. The same player did the damage in the 51st minute. Ernie Taylor, who would soon join Blackpool, neatly laid the ball back into the striker's path and his shot from outside the area flew into the corner of the net. Blackpool worked hard for a goal to get back into the game, but the best chance again fell to Milburn whose header nearly brought him a hat-trick. The Seasiders had been well beaten and there could be few complaints.

Brown recalls: "Although I was out with injury, I went to the match and it was a good occasion. It gave me an insight into what went on. I was in the dressing-room during the build-up and then sat on the touchline. Once Jackie Milburn blasted a shot in I thought we were going to lose. I was obviously disappointed to miss out and then sorry for the lads when we lost. I don't think any of us could imagine we would be back again in two years."

Blackpool had again failed at the final hurdle, but at a dinner at the Café Royal, London, Harry Evans, the club's chairman, reminded the audience and the press of how far the club had come in a short space of time. A Bloomfield Road ground that once held 22,000 now had a 32,000 capacity. A young team – and a still young enough Stanley Matthews – had shown it could compete at the highest level in the game and would ensure a glorious future for the club. He added: "Our ambition as a club is to give Blackpool, a comparatively small provincial town, football worthy of the town's reputation as an entertainment centre. I think we've succeeded."

Manager Joe Smith thought the occasion was probably too much for some of the younger players, but he was not going to criticise them. Rather he thanked them for bringing the club so far. And he added: "We're proud to have gone to Wembley twice in three years. We hope to be there again next year – and don't be surprised if we are. We'll make some team sit up yet." His prophecy was to be only slightly wide of the mark.

Back on the Wembley Trail

MANAGER Joe Smith's prediction in the aftermath of defeat in 1951 that his side would return to Wembley the following year proved wide of the mark. But only just. It was, in fact, to be two seasons later when the Seasiders went back to the Twin Towers to face Bolton Wanderers. They had the nation urging them on as almost everyone outside of Bolton hoped Stanley Matthews would gain his Cup winners' medal. The match proved to be one of the most famous the old stadium has ever seen.

The 1951-52 season had brought disappointment. All sides hope to bounce back from a Wembley defeat by returning the following year and making right the wrong. "We'll be back next year," is a mantra repeated by players and fans alike. Yet Blackpool didn't get past the first hurdle with a trip to West Ham United, a mid-table Second Division side, proving too tough a challenge as they lost 2-1. Matthews himself always believed it was asking too much of a team to get back to Wembley in successive years, although as if to contradict him Newcastle would return and successfully defend the Cup by beating Arsenal.

In the League, Blackpool's form was mediocre and although ninth place was hardly a disgrace, it was much less than the fans had hoped for. One highlight was the visit of Newcastle United and the chance for revenge for the Cup defeat. It produced the highest score of the season with a 6-3 win. Overall, the League results were not helped with both Matthews and Jackie Mudie being sidelined for a large part of the season with injuries. In the case of Matthews, many were starting to question whether he would be back although the player himself found it a source of irritation at this time that the pundits were always quick to end his career for him.

The following year, fortunes in the League were little better and Blackpool finished seventh. This time, though, few cared. The Seasiders were back on the Wembley trail again. First up was First Division opposition in the shape of Sheffield Wednesday, but the Blackpool team successfully made the trip to Yorkshire returning with a 2-1 win. Matthews made his return after a long lay off with an injury that required an operation. Again people were talking of the England man in the past tense and wondering whether his playing days were drawing to a close. As he so often did, he confounded his critics. Although never a prolific scorer, Matthews got the first goal to herald his return.

The second goal was scored by a player who Blackpool fans had been cursing at Wembley two seasons before, but who had quickly become a favourite with the Bloomfield Road faithful. It was rumoured that it was at the express wish of Matthews himself that the inside-right Ernie Taylor was signed from Newcastle United. He joined for the princely sum of £25,000 and stayed for seven seasons, making 242 appearances and scoring 55 goals.

He teamed up brilliantly with Matthews on the right and his accurate passes gave the master perfect service. He played only once at full international level and had the misfortune to make his debut when the Hungarians were handing out a football lesson and after the 6-3 defeat he never wore the white shirt of England again. He left Blackpool in the wake of the Munich air disaster to join Manchester United, for whom he appeared in the 1958 FA Cup Final.

Huddersfield Town, who would that season win promotion to Division One, were the visitors for the fourth-round tie and they were to depart from the competition thanks to a freak goal by the Blackpool full-back Tommy Garrett. He hit a high speculative effort from inside his own half that lobbed into the net and proved to be the only goal of the match. Garrett was working down the pit at Horden Colliery when he was signed by Blackpool in 1942. Powerful in the air, he also had footballing skills not always in evidence in defenders of this era. He played in the 1951 Final and would again be on show in 1953, despite having suffered a broken nose the week before. He was a loyal servant of the club for 19 years before departing to Millwall on a free transfer in May 1961, where he played only a dozen games before retiring.

Bill Perry remembers the Huddersfield game, saying: "In the Cup you need a little bit of luck along the way if you are going to get to Wembley. The game was played in a gale and it was a great leveller, although to be honest we didn't play well. Tommy Garrett lobbed the ball from defence hoping to find Morty, but because of the strong wind the goalkeeper ran out and misjudged the ball and it bounced into the net. It was a bit of luck just when we needed it. That was the biggest bit of good fortune we had in the entire Cup run. When you get a break like that then, as a player, you start to think that this might be your year."

Another Second Division side, Southampton, were the visitors in the fifth round and the south coast outfit had centre-forward and top goalscorer Frank Dudley leading the attack after missing a League match the previous week with a stomach complaint. It was at least some good news for a side that were 10-1 against to win and whose manager George Roughton was relying on the vagaries of the Cup as much as anything to see his side through. The former Huddersfield Town and Manchester United player was taking the philosophical view that there was nothing to lose and everything to win. It may well have been a touch of gamesmanship because on the day his side game perilously close to an upset.

Southampton's performance was never pretty but as befits the underdogs in the Cup-tie, they battled hard and gave away nothing. Certainly they were never overawed by the galaxy of talent that had taken the field against them. Blackpool could not create many chances against the massed ranks of red-and-white striped defenders. The home side's only goal came in the 62nd minute when Bill Perry took advantage of some rare space provided by the visitors. Now a goal behind, Southampton abandoned Plan A, the massed defence, and adopted Plan B, an aggressive attack, and it brought its reward. A huge lofted pass from inside their own half was met by the head of Henry Horton. It meant a replay at The Dell and the odds on a Southampton victory had suddenly and dramatically been cut.

Blackpool travelled south knowing that the quarter-final draw had pitched the winner of this replay into a tie at Highbury against a powerful Arsenal side, who were Finalists the year before. First, though, they needed to overcome the Saints before a near-capacity 30,000 crowd and it was never going to be easy. Dudley missed an easy chance in the opening minutes when, with only Farm to beat, he fired over the bar. It was, though, the home side who took the lead after 17 minutes when John Walker played a one-two with John Hoskins and saw his first shot blocked but made no mistake with the rebound. Southampton were not allowing the visitors to settle into their rhythm and it was looking like an uphill fight. At half-time Blackpool were still trailing, but four minutes after the interval they had taken the lead. Horton, the hero of the previous match, deflected a Perry shot past his own goalkeeper and two minutes later Allan Brown scored what proved the winner.

There were 68,000 packed into Highbury and touts who would normally only be in business for the semi-finals and Final of the FA Cup were asking £5 for a 12s 6d (63p) ticket for what was a mouthwatering match that pitted two of the country's top teams against each other, with the additional bonus of the great Stanley Matthews on display. In keeping with their recent Cup tradition it was the Seasiders who triumphed, but they paid a price. In scoring the winning goal in a 2-1 victory, Allan Brown suffered a broken left leg that ensured for the second time running he would miss out on a trip to Wembley. It was said that afterwards the captain Harry Johnston declared he would rather have seen the match go to a replay than lose Brown in such circumstances in the final few minutes.

An Arsenal team hailed as the best in the land, and who would go on to win the League title, were outclassed by a Blackpool side that reached glittering heights on the day. Ernie Taylor and the Arsenal playmaker Jimmy Logie had both scored before Brown, the outstanding forward on the day, scored the winner with only minutes remaining and at such a huge personal cost. His goal guaranteed a semi-final place against Tottenham Hotspur, who came through a replay to beat Birmingham City. The player himself, though, would take no further part in the season's proceedings. To have missed one Cup Final through injury was unfortunate but two was a cruel blow. To add insult to injury, the broken leg probably cost him a Scottish cap as the national selectors had been at Highbury and were reportedly pleased with what they saw the inside-forward produce on the day.

Looking back on a career that spanned three decades at Blackpool, Hugh Kelly is clear on one issue: "The Arsenal game was the best I ever took part in. It was the best performance Blackpool produced while I was with them. The Gunners were on top form and were a great side, but we were better. The only thing that spoiled the day was Allan Brown breaking his leg. The Arsenal goalkeeper Jack Kelsey fell across him as he scored the winning goal. We heard the crack as his leg broke, all over the ground. It was that dramatic. There's no question it was an accident. We knew he was going to miss the Final and he had already missed out in 1951. He also missed out on playing for Scotland. He was very unlucky. There was still a semi-final to go but the way we were playing we thought it was our year for a Wembley trip"

Brown himself can remember the incident. The cross from Matthews, his effort to lift the ball over the goalkeeper, the challenge from the diving goalkeeper and the moment of agony when his leg was broken. Later would come the despair when he realised that for the second time he would miss out on a Wembley Final. On the big day itself he would again be cheering from the touchline. He admits there were, of course, pangs of regret, but they were mixed with the elation of the historic win.

Bill Perry is in no doubt that the team excelled itself that day. In the run up to the League game between the sides, which was played the week before the historic Cup quarter-final, one famous newspaper writer of the day had predicted an Arsenal win because they had been on a good run of form prior to the match and had beaten Blackpool at Highbury earlier in the season. The Gunners unbeaten League run ended in a 3-2 defeat at Bloomfield Road. The Arsenal captain Joe Mercer had poked his head around the door after the game and as he left he said: "We'll get you next week. It will be a different story altogether."

Yet the League win proved a psychological boost to the side for the Cup-tie, believes Perry. "The game itself was an exciting, ding-dong, hard-fought match that must have been marvellous entertainment for the spectators. Matthews and Morty were on top of their game. In fact, all 22 players gave everything in that game. Arsenal were determined to avenge the League defeat and progress in the Cup and you could say we were fortunate in the end to have won because it was very even with nothing to choose between the sides. Allan Brown's sacrifice to score the goal saw us through, but cost him his place. We only had time to go back to the centre-circle and the ref blew his whistle. It was that late a goal to decide the issue. It was very sad for Allan. The Final was played six weeks after the semi, yet everybody knew whatever the outcome against Spurs he was going to miss another trip to Wembley because of the injury."

Spurs as the opposition provided a re-run of the 1948 semi-final in which the Seasiders triumphed 3-1 after extra-time. This time the London club were in the First rather than Second Division and the task at Villa Park was likely to be much harder. The other semi-final pitted Bolton Wanderers against Everton at Maine Road. More than 68,000 would be in Birmingham to see if Blackpool could make it third time lucky in the Cup.

The Lancashire side did progress, but neutrals in the ground were of the opinion they had been fortunate. Spurs showed the greater skills, had much of the best attacking play and combined together well, yet in the all-important finishing department it was Blackpool who had the vital edge. Blackpool had Mortensen on a rare off-day and were undoubtedly missing Brown. Yet with the game tied it was the men in tangerine who made the best efforts to find a winner and it duly came.

Perry recalls "That year I got a lot of satisfaction out of the Cup-ties leading up to the Final. I had scored in the semi in 1951 and was to do so again this time. I scored the opening goal from a Matthews corner, but the lead lasted only around 20 minutes before they equalised. I got injured playing against Alf Ramsey. He was a good player but I always seemed to do quite well against him. I was something of a passenger as the game wore on. Ramsey attempted a pass back to the goalkeeper with five minutes to go and Jackie Mudie intercepted and scored the winning goal. It had been another close game but I think beforehand everybody was aware we weren't going to miss out. We would be going to Wembley and this time we would lift the Cup."

The team had proved themselves something of 11th-hour specialists at snatching Cup-ties in the closing stages of this campaign. Three times the crucial goal came in the dying minutes: Taylor scored with two minutes left against Sheffield, Garrett with seven minutes remaining against Huddersfield, and Brown struck in the 88th minute at Arsenal. Now in the last minute of ordinary time Jackie Mudie profited from a bad mistake by Ramsey to book a place at Wembley. Minutes before, chances had been saved but this proved decisive. At the back Johnston turned in a captain's performance to keep a powerful front line in check.

With their place at Wembley assured, Kelly was to suffer the crushing blow all players dread. There was often criticism voiced that the gap between the semi-final and the Final was too long. In 1953, the semi was on March 21 with the Final not being played until May 2. Too often the form of teams involved at Wembley suffers because of the distraction of the big day ahead. For some individuals, injury can deprive them of their place on the historic day. So it was to be for Kelly.

He takes up the story: "It was the last home game of the season and we were playing Liverpool with nothing at stake for either team in the League. They had a big forward called Louis Bimpson. I was going to pick the ball up as it was over the line and he hit me on the ankle. I finished the game all right but later that night it started throbbing until the pain was unbearable. I phoned the trainer and he told me to take something and try and get a couple of hours sleep. He collected me at 6am the following morning. The verdict of the specialist was that the bone was cracked. I was joining Allan Brown on the sidelines for the Final."

The Matthews Final

W ITH a month to go to the big match on May 2, 1953, the groundswell of opinion that this should be the occasion when Stanley Matthews finally got his winners' medal was already starting to build and Bolton players and fans had only to glance at the national newspapers to see how the idea of a 'Stanley Matthews Final' was being built up. The player himself was inundated with fan mail and good wishes on his third attempt at being on a winning side at Wembley. In the town itself there was a firm conviction that this would be the legendary player's year and his medal collection would be completed.

Blackpool could certainly rely on experience of the unique atmosphere of Wembley. Four players had been with the team in their two previous visits in 1948 and 1951. They were the two Stans, Matthews and Mortensen, the captain Harry Johnston and full-back Eddie Shimwell. Only the young half-backs, Ewan Fenton and Cyril Robinson, had not been at an FA Cup Final. It was hoped that such experience would prove a crucial factor on the day. And, of course, Ernie Taylor had been there with Newcastle.

There was also a feeling that if the side had enjoyed a smooth passage to the Final on their previous two visits, this time they had arrived the hard way with some tough encounters, not least away wins at Sheffield Wednesday and Arsenal and a last-gasp semi-final victory against Spurs.

The crowds were again at Central Station in Blackpool to see the team depart with around 2,000 cheering and wishing the side well. The last football the chosen 12 had taken part in was a six-a-side kickabout in Stanley Park the day before. It had been decided not to go to an out-of-town venue in the run-up to the Final and it was on the Friday that the team left the town for an Elizabethan manor house in Elstree, London. Manager Joe Smith told the crowd that he hoped they wouldn't be disappointed, but if they were, it would not be for the want of his team trying. The arrival of the team invalids, Allan Brown and Hugh Kelly, prompted a moment's silence before a huge cheer went up in their honour. Many watching must have feared the impact on the team the loss of two such outstanding players would have.

The Bolton players had also decided to stay at home rather than go to an out-of-town training camp in the build-up to the Final. They worked out at Burnden before, on the Thursday before the match, heading for Hendon, North London, where the squad was to be based. The players were calm and confident on the morning of the match. Nat Lofthouse recalls that the key instruction from manager Bill Ridding was to try to dictate play.

The phone at Syd Bevers' home had never stopped ringing with would-be Atomic Boys keen to join the troupe, knowing it guaranteed a ticket. They were the official mascots of the club and also generated publicity for the town. This was the year the pre-match build-up included a visit to Number 10 Downing Street with a stick of rock. Yet during the match itself, Bevers remembers even the Atomic Boys struggled to keep their spirits high as it appeared it would be another Wembley disappointment for Blackpool. But thanks to a marvellous finish, it would be the men in tangerine and white suits who would be leading the celebrations in London's West End.

Ticket touts who usually profited from such occasions were reporting their worst year in decades. And it was no reflection on the drawing power of the match. Rather the northern fans were refusing to part with their tickets at any price, such was the interest in the game. The rules of supply and demand were overthrown. There were no tickets to supply, however great the demand. When there was a spare ticket, and it was a rare event, the Lancashire fans were happy to keep it among their own. One man searching for a genuine football fan to sell him a 10s 6d (53p) ticket at face value was thrilled when he found one and his place for the big match was assured.

An injury doubt concerning Stanley Matthews was one of the best-kept secrets in the run up to the Final. While playing in a six-a-side game at Stanley Park he felt pain in his thigh. A couple of hours before the big game he was given an injection for the muscle problem to numb the pain and ensure his speed was not affected. The injury would be serious enough to force him to turn down an invitation to join the FA squad on a month-long tour of South America that was leaving the following week.

The build-up to the Final had been a difficult time for Hugh Kelly and Allan Brown as they hobbled about on their crutches. Kelly said: "The whole build-up was a long, drawn-out affair. We both agreed that if it ever happened again we would request the club let us travel down on the Saturday on our own. It was embarrassing being in the hotel during the build-up. Allan and I felt so far out of it, which was only natural. We were walking about on crutches while everybody else was getting ready. I wouldn't recommend any player to go through it. In a way, because I had played in two Finals, missing out wasn't as much of a blow as it might have been, though."

The weather was perfect and the conditions ideal as the players lined up to be introduced to Prince Philip. The stadium was packed, of course, and Bolton were in a mood to ruin Matthews' big day. Within two minutes of the start they were in the lead with a goal from Nat Lofthouse from 20 yards out on the right after a quick pass inside by Doug Holden, although the shot was not as powerful as it might have been and Farm in the Blackpool goal should have saved. Lofthouse had succeeded in the not inconsiderable feat of scoring in every round of the competition. Blackpool settled, but the goal had given the Wanderers confidence and they worked hard to extend the lead.

For Bolton, injury doubts before the game surrounding Eric Bell were now confirmed. It meant an enforced change of positions with Bobby Langton moving to inside-left, Bell taking over from him at outside-left and Harold Hassall dropping into the left-half position vacated by Bell. After the changes it was to be Blackpool who scored next through Stan Mortensen, whose shot was helped by a Hassall deflection. They were not on level terms for long, though, as a 39th-minute goal for Willie Moir gave Bolton a half-time lead. The general consensus was that it was a poor first half with nerves perhaps taking their toll.

Yet Lofthouse recalls an incident which he believes sums up the nature of the game in this era. At half-time, Mortensen shook his hand and congratulated him on scoring in every round, a piece of sportsmanship that it is hard to imagine being repeated half-way through a Cup Final in this day and age. Five years before, of course, it was the Blackpool player who had achieved the feat. Injury had kept him out in the early rounds of this Cup run. Now Morty would show his pedigree to devastating effect.

In the dressing-room, Bill Perry remembers the general feeling being that although they were losing, there was little to choose between the teams and Blackpool were certainly in contention. The players were aware that the injury to Bell effectively reduced the opposition to ten men and it was hoped they could profit as the game wore on. There were no great tactical plans or new strategies planned. Everybody knew what was needed.

Bolton's workmanlike approach was giving them the edge over Blackpool's neater passing moves and in the 55th minute the injured Bell remarkably scored their third when he got his head to a Holden cross. That the Bolton man was able to get to the ball was, in the view of Eddie Hopkinson, the future Bolton and England goalkeeper, nothing short of incredible. He was with the party for the day, but was not yet a first-teamer.

Bolton fans Fred and Florence Guest had booked into the Russell Hotel on Russell Square in the heart of London and were making a weekend of the Final because Fred did a lot of business in London. Their daughter was not interested in the game, but had driven them to the match, only to find herself surrounded by policemen eager to listen to the action unfold on the radio. With Bolton in a comfortable lead, a fellow guest at the hotel now tapped Florence on the shoulder and promised champagne back at the hotel. The celebrations were already being planned by the Bolton contingent. It was to prove premature. Florence remembers Stanley Matthews delivering from right in front of them the cross that was to decide the contest. The player fell as he made contact, but the ball was still accurately delivered. Although it meant defeat, she can remember being mesmerised by the skill of the Blackpool winger dribbling the ball as only he could.

She said: "We had lost and it was all through Stanley Matthews. We were sorry to have lost, but Matthews was so popular and admired we thought that if we had to be beaten we were glad it was Blackpool. We were good losers. If it had been another side I might have been more upset. And it was a Lancashire derby. We still went back and celebrated and when we opened the champagne we toasted Stanley Matthews. It was Stan who had won."

Hopkinson, as befits a goalkeeper, has sympathy for Stan Hanson who was in goal for Wanderers. The 66th-minute goal by Mortensen came when Hanson failed to hold a Matthews cross and the centre-forward pounced, pushing the ball just inside the post. "I've read and talked about that game for the past 40-odd years," says Hopkinson, "and it was quite remarkable although Stanley Matthews only took part in the last 20 minutes. He had done bugger-all up until then. Hanson had a good pair of hands, but when he let a Matthews cross through and Mortensen knocked it in, that was the beginning of the end. I know Hanson was upset about the goal because he was normally so reliable. It was one of the few times he made a mistake and you could say it cost Bolton the Cup. I know he certainly felt that way."

Certainly Perry remembers that the mistake by Hanson was the piece of good fortune the Blackpool side needed to get back into the game and it gave the side a much-needed lift. Yet it was not a good game for goalkeepers all round. George Farm had been culpable in two of the Bolton goals. However, victory helped the lapses slip from the fans' memory. The player himself said: "I would not have known what to do with myself if we had lost, for I made some stupid mistakes. I don't know what went wrong with me. I suppose it was just that it was the Cup Final. Anyway, the lads did a fine job."

Yet another verdict on the crucial turning point in the match is delivered by Tommy Banks, who was also watching from the sidelines with the Bolton camp and who would become a regular for Wanderers and play for England. Although all are agreed on the significance of Bell's injury, the number of dramatic moments highlighted by the watching professionals is proof of what an exciting contest the game was. In Banks' view, Doug Holden was Bolton's best player on the field and was unlucky to have been penalised for a tackle in a dangerous position for Wanderers. So it proved. Mortensen's shot from the free-kick, three yards outside the penalty area, beat the unsighted Hanson and provided Blackpool's equaliser.

Sitting on the touchline, a disappointed Roy Hartle of Bolton remembers thinking that although he had missed out on getting on to the pitch for the biggest game of his career, there was at least the consolation of the £25 win bonus because the team looked well on course for victory. The Bolton man had been dropped for the Final after playing in every round. Then it all went to pieces. He has no complaints about Bell declaring himself fit after his injury a few weeks earlier. As he says, many other players given the chance of a place in the Cup Final would have done the same. Crucially, though, it meant Bolton were down to ten men.

So just as it looked as if the Cup would be heading back to Bolton, the most memorable events unfolded. The Mortensen goal capitalising on Hanson's mistake put the Seasiders back into contention. Until this point, Matthews had been kept relatively quiet but with defenders tiring, particularly having to cover for the injured Bell, it was now that the veteran winger worked his magic and drew on all his vast experience. Suddenly the crosses started to be fired over and it was only a matter of time before Mortensen scored and completed his hat-trick. The public may have dedicated the match to Matthews, but the player himself is in no doubt as he said in his own book *The Stanley Matthews Story*: "Anyone who scores a hat-trick in a Cup Final is the man of the match."

Hartle recalls: "The thing I can remember was Stan. He was destroying everyone. I felt sorry for Ralph Banks who was struggling to deal with him. It was as though the thought had crossed Stan's mind that this was his last chance. If he didn't do it now, that was the end."

Bolton were now under pressure and with only a few minutes left to play, it was their opponents who were going all out for the winner. Perry says: "At 3-2 I was thinking that if we got another goal we could take the game into extra-time. Now Mortensen's shot that was crashed into the net had given us renewed enthusiasm and we went all out for the winner. The goal was a huge boost to us. They were playing with ten men and it was starting to take its toll. Both Stan Matthews and I had been having a quiet game up until the last minutes. Now Stan was firing the crosses over."

With a minute to go, Matthews controlled the ball and raced away, beating two defenders as the crowd urged him on. He centred, falling as he did so, and the ball went past the waiting Morty and landed at the feet of Bill Perry who fired home the winning goal. Yet Perry admits: "I got greater personal satisfaction from the games leading up to the Final rather than the Final itself. I didn't have one of my best games. I was up against John Ball who was a good player. When the Matthews cross came over, I happened to be in the right spot at the right time. I was round about the penalty-spot and I let fly with my right foot and I can't tell you how pleased I was to see the ball hit the back of the net. There were a lot of players in the goalmouth and it could so easily have been deflected. The whistle blew a couple of minutes later. What a difference the experience was to 1951. I'd had the experience of losing and now I could enjoy the feeling of elation at winning. We had won the FA Cup. It was particularly special for Stanley Matthews because he had won virtually very other honour in the game except the Cup Final winners' medal. The whole country was behind us."

Many not fortunate to be at Wembley can still remember the commentary by the BBC's Raymond Glendenning as the game reached its climax. "...Taylor to Matthews on the right...Matthews beats one man, beats two...moves in...he centres...it's Perry...Perry has scored, Perry has scored!" Matthews had his medal and the Bolton players were left with only heartbreak. In his book *Goals Galore* Lofthouse confesses: "When I reached the dressing-room I broke down for the first time since I was a boy and wept unashamedly. Even the champagne we had brought with us to Wembley tasted bitter."

Another figure on the touchline was Hugh Kelly and he reflects: "At one stage I had given it up then suddenly Blackpool came to life. We were working the ball down the right from defence, through to Taylor, then to Matthews and that was the danger for Bolton and I could see them start to get rattled. I started to think there was a chance for a draw and it came and then I thought we would have a chance in extra-time, only for Matthews to push the ball through to Perry and that was it. After that game I think the Bolton players must have put their heads under the cold tap to come round. They just couldn't believe it had happened."

Ray Hall had failed to get a ticket but the family of a friend who lived nearby had a television and they all crammed into the small lounge to watch the game on a tiny black and white screen. "When the final whistle went everybody poured out of the sweaty living room, and in the road a bus with a huge tangerine rosette on the front of it had stopped and the driver was out of his cab and going mental, jumping up and down. I still don't know how he got to hear the score so quickly. We all just joined in the celebrations."

For yet another perspective on why it all went wrong for Bolton, Malcolm Barrass, the Bolton centre-half, highlights another key figure in the Blackpool revival to go alongside Matthews and Mortensen. He believes a turning point was the passing skills of Ernie Taylor, who began to provide the winger with a wonderful service. Early on, the Bolton defenders were successful at keeping Matthews quiet, but he was now getting perfect passes.

He adds: "It had been a harum-scarum Cup run and we were all glad to be at Wembley. We were all friends together and it is a good occasion to share. We all played our hardest on the field and then went for a pint with the Blackpool lads after. We might have been enemies on the pitch, but when the referee blew the final whistle we were all old pals again." Later in the evening, crowds packed outside the Café Royal, where the after-match dinner was being held, would hear three rousing cheers. It was the Blackpool players paying tribute to their worthy opponents who had been such good losers.

After being on the losing side in the 1951 Final and kicking the turf in desperation, Matthews had vowed to himself that he would return one day. As he said in his book *The Stanley Matthews Story*, once the after-match furore was over and the Cup had been paraded around the ground and the interviews and photographs were completed, he changed, quietly left the dressing-room, and made his way back up the tunnel and on to the pitch.

"The vast stadium was now deserted. I walked to the spot where I had kicked the turf at the end of the 1951 Final, looked up in the sky, and held out the medal in the palm of my hand – it was the only way I could think of to show it to my father. As I held out my medal, the sun came from behind a small cloud and shone down on it. Standing there, a wonderful feeling of peace entered my mind and body. I felt that all the years from boyhood to manhood in football finished here. I had fulfilled my destiny."

Tommy Banks couldn't resist a quick word with the great Matthews who had so tormented his brother on the field in the dying stages of the game, and when the winger had returned from his reflections, there was Tommy. "I said to Stan that we wouldn't have lost if I had played, but it never bothered Stan one little bit. He didn't care. He had his medal and he was never fazed anyway. I was a bit of a rabbit for him, though. I don't know why, but I always had a fair game against him. He was still a ghost on the field though."

And Tommy is happy to put an end to a popular myth among Bolton supporters that Matthews used to cry-off from games at Burnden Park, fearing the infamous gravel rash from a Tommy Banks tackle that would pitch him on to the track that ran around the ground. Sadly, it's nonsense. As Tommy says, Matthews wasn't afraid of anything or anyone on a football field.

Kelly believes many players deserve their share of the accolades for the win and not just Matthews. Indeed, he knows Stan himself always wanted it that way. There was the finishing of Mortensen, the passing skills of Taylor and the general all-round fighting spirit that played their part. "The papers called it the Matthews Final because he had been there twice and not collected a winners' medal, but I thought it was all wrong for it to be described in that way. There were others in the team that had been to Wembley twice before. By all means recognise he gave the winning pass, but remember it all started somewhere else. Stan was embarrassed, but it's what happened. The papers started it all."

For both Kelly and Brown there were special medals struck and Kelly remembers it took some persuading before the FA agreed to mint the extra medals. It means with his collection he can study how the designs changed over the five years. They are his prized possessions and have been through the years. He has three daughters and in time each will inherit one.

At the after-match banquet, the Bolton captain Willie Moir felt the game had been lost because the match was five minutes too long and his players were exhausted, having run themselves into the ground. Certainly injuries took their toll, with Bell a virtual passenger for much of the game and at various times Lofthouse and Ralph Banks also off the field receiving treatment. There was a feeling expressed that when Matthews began to weave his magic at the expense of Banks, there should have been a reshuffle with Banks swopping wings with the fitter and in-form Ball. Hindsight, though, is a wonderful thing.

Harry Johnston said that even when the side were 3-1 down he was still convinced that the game could be won. He couldn't imagine returning to Blackpool empty-handed for the third time in five years. To have achieved the win in the Queen's Coronation Year and to have received the Cup from her was the proudest moment of his life. There was also a special mention for Allan Brown and Hugh Kelly who had suffered the misery of being injured and missing the greatest day in Blackpool's football history.

The Mid-1950s

THE two seasons after the glory of their Wembley win brought out the best and worst in the Blackpool side. In 1953-54 they finished sixth in the League to underline their status as one of the leading teams in the country. Yet the following campaign was an aberration. It marked their lowest point in the decade and, astonishingly, brought the spectre of relegation to Bloomfield Road. It was, though, to prove a temporary lapse.

Win, lose or draw, the Atomic Boys were there to support the team in their own inimitable way. As Syd Bevers says, the travelling troupe of supporters were now famous around the country. He would write to the various clubs before they were due to play there to ask permission to put the duck on the centre-circle. They travelled long distances to offer their dedicated support. The duck made his appearance at grounds from Hampden Park to The Dell. There were few famous grounds not entertained by the Atomic Boys and Puskas. Over the years they travelled, only two clubs refused permission – Leeds United and Huddersfield Town.

It was only at the home games that there was the full parade of the pitch. The Boys' retinue had now grown. A clown and stilt walker from Tower Circus were in the procession along with Laurel and Hardy look-alikes and a 6ft 7ins bloke dressed as a wartime ATS girl. They competed to out-do one another. These were still the glory days for Blackpool. The attendance figures were healthy and for the 1953-54 season at least, the results were good. The team was not compromising, either, on its reputation for playing attractive attacking football.

With the euphoria of the Cup win not yet abated, Blackpool made a determined assault on the League title and won four of their five opening games. Until mid-November the team were in contention then with injuries taking their toll, the Seasiders hit a slump that effectively cost them any chance of the title. They went ten games without a win. It was a trip to Old Trafford where they suffered a 4-1 reverse against Manchester United that began the disappointing spell and it was not until January 23 and the visit of Aston Villa that they ended the dismal run of form with a 3-2 victory. The side ended the campaign with a flourish to ensure a high finish in the table and restore confidence that the good times would remain. It included a 3-0 home win against Liverpool to close another season.

Hopes of retaining the Cup, though, were to be shattered in humiliating fashion. A four-match marathon with Second Division Luton Town that went to two neutral venues was eventually decided at Molineux with a 2-0 win, courtesy of Perry and Len Stephenson. It produced a fourth-round tie against another Second Division side, West Ham United. The Seasiders travelled to Upton Park and secured a 1-1 draw with Allan Brown, now fully recovered from his injury, collecting the goal for the Lancashire side. It earned a replay at Bloomfield Road and on a frost-bound pitch that was left deeply rutted in places, it was the South African Perry who proved decisive as he raced around seemingly impervious to the conditions. The groundstaff had cleared an estimated 100 tons of snow off the playing surface in a 24-hour operation before kick-off. While his opposing full-back was wary of the treacherous nature of the turf, Perry was happy to take advantage. A shot in the 29th minute opened the Blackpool account. He was on target in the 70th minute and provided the pass for Brown to make it three. The Londoners could manage just one in return against a resolute defence and Farm at his best in goal.

After struggling through the first two rounds, the draw now threw up Third Division North opposition in the shape of Port Vale and a quarter-final place looked there for the taking. The unpredictability of the Cup, though, was about to come to the fore. It produced the sort of game that makes the First Division side and its supporters despair, but yet which has neutrals lauding the magic of the competition. For the players of lowly Vale – albeit they were going to storm away with the Northern Section title this season – it was their chance to bask in the limelight.

Nearly 8,000 fans had made the journey to the Potteries, convinced they would see their side triumph. Yet Blackpool's Cup hopes were to sink without a trace in the thick mud of Vale Park. The lower division side raised their game to heights that must have surprised even them and they were helped in their cause by a lacklustre display by the visitors who seemed devoid of ideas and any sort of battling qualities. The conditions were a great leveller to be sure. But this was an occasion for rolling up shirt sleeves and getting stuck in. There was little time for fancy football. Hard tackles and accurate long passes were what was required and what was lacking from the Seasiders. Farm failed to reach a centre and Albert Leake had the first Vale goal. Against a well-marshalled defence, Stan Matthews had a bad day with his control and passes not of the usual quality. The second goal of the game again went to Vale and again it was Leake who was the scorer. It was the last of the match and Vale had won a comfortable and remarkable victory. The Third Division side eventually reached the sem-finals where they lost to West Bromwich Albion, eventual winners of the trophy in a Final against Preston.

Allan Brown blames the conditions when he looks back on the defeat that caused dismay in the town. He said: "It was pouring with rain and as muddy as anything. Those conditions benefited a team that boots the ball up the field and chases after it. That was how they got away with a win. It was hard to play football in the conditions and, to be fair, we also had an off-day. They had the game for the conditions, which were a great leveller. When we got back it was hard to live down having been beaten by a Third Division side when we were the Cup holders. We were all disappointed as well as the supporters."

Peter Collins was one of the fans who had joined the exodus from

Blackpool for the match. They travelled in high hopes, convinced that there would be another trip to Wembley for the side that had proved itself the leading exponents of Cup football. He said: "I'm sure fans asked to remember the most disappointing games from this era will come up with this one. There was no argument we would win the game. Thousands had made the journey to the Midlands. It was a horrible day and the pitch was terrible, the terracing was awful. We just didn't believe the condition of the ground. We didn't get beaten in those days by a side like Vale, but we did that day and we couldn't believe it. The journey back was a long one."

Such disappointments in League and Cup were to return in the 1954-55 season, and with interest. A shocking run of results meant that relegation seemed assured until a dramatic late fightback. Yet the personnel were largely the same. The team would return to winning ways the following season. It was a mystery to players and fans alike. Certainly old campaigners Harry Johnston and Stan Mortensen were not getting any younger. Neither was Stan Matthews and he would miss a few games through injury, but certainly not as many as in previous campaigns when the side had coped. Yet to go from title challengers to this was little short of amazing.

Perry says: "Since I'd arrived in 1949 we were always high in the League. I think the fans and even the players had come to expect it, which was why this season was such a surprise. A lot of the forwards were out for various parts of the season. I think I missed half a dozen games late on and most of the others had spells out with injury. Having players missing upsets the balance in the side. Nowadays the top clubs have 22 players who can play first-team football. If anybody is missing they can step in because they are close in standard to the regular first-team player. In those days that wasn't the case. There was a big gap between first-team players and the reserves. At Blackpool during this season there were not the quality of players to call on."

He adds that the malaise was obviously short-term as the following year, with a squad largely untroubled by injuries, they reached the runners-up spot in the top flight. Indeed, he feels the side came desperately close to winning the title but for a poor finish to the season. It underlined the need to keep an unchanged team. In the days before any sort of squad system, there was no rotation of the first team. The same players would be on the team sheet for year after year unless they were injured. With their best team out, the Seasiders were still a match for anyone.

Hugh Kelly remembers: "I have no idea why it all went so wrong that season. We went from the top to the bottom in one year and with the same players. There was no reason why it should have been such a bad season. There were a few injuries but nothing that we shouldn't have been able to handle. Results didn't go right and I suppose it was just one of those things. Happily, we bounced back."

Allan Brown adds: "You only need a few injuries to key players and a run of results to go against you, and doubts start to creep in. We were a good side when we were all together, but once things started to go wrong we didn't seem able to turn it round. I don't know why. Normally we didn't fear anybody with the players we had, but that season things just didn't happen for us."

After travelling across the Pennines and winning their opening fixture with a 3-1 victory at Huddersfield Town, it was a disastrous slump for the side. The Seasiders could manage only one win in their next dozen games and only two draws. Such a run left them deep in the relegation zone. A 1-0 victory over Chelsea on October 23 sparked a mini-revival that saw them suffer only one defeat in ten games, but then it was back to the horror days of the start of the season with five defeats in the next six games. With three games of the season left, there was still a danger of the drop, but an impressive 6-1 victory over Manchester City at Maine Road relieved the danger. There was a hat-trick for Perry and a brace for Mortensen, with Brown also getting in on the act to bring back memories of the Blackpool of old.

In their last 13 games, there were only three defeats and one of those was a last-game-of-the-season reverse against Sheffield United when the club were already safe. Such a run of form at the beginning of the campaign would have had the fans thinking of a top-four finish. As it was, the return to winning ways showed that the worst was behind the team and it paved the way for the following season when such consistency would be maintained.

Yet in the middle of their worst spell of form in the League, the draw for the third round of the Cup saw Third Division North side York City visit Bloomfield Road on January 3. Two days before, on New Year's Day, Manchester United had inflicted a morale-sapping 4-1 defeat at Old Trafford. The scene was set for one of the great Cup shocks of the post-war years. To lose away from home and when the conditions are a leveller is a crushing blow but can, just about, be forgiven. Now on their own turf the First Division side would be outplayed to the delight of the 7,000 fans who had made the journey across the Pennines. Many had come as much for a day on the Golden Mile as the game itself, hardly believing they could humble the mighty Blackpool, who boasted both Matthews and Mortensen in their ranks.

Allan Brown takes a philosophical view saying: "After the Port Vale defeat the season before, this was the last thing we needed. I was sitting on the bench and, naturally enough, the crowd were discontent that we were getting beaten by York City. There were no real excuses. It was just one of those times when we had an off-day and they played out of their skins. It's the sort of thing that happens in Cup runs. It's just not very nice when it is happening to you."

The official verdict was that this was one of the worst displays by a Blackpool forward line that anyone could remember and that they failed to score was no surprise. The home cause was not helped, either, by a missed penalty by Jim Kelly. York played a simple, direct game and reaped the benefits with goals for Sid Storey and Billy Fenton. The Seasiders could not even claim to have been unlucky or been physically bullied out of the match. The truth is they were outplayed. And like Port Vale before them, York went all the way to the semi-finals where they lost to the eventual Cup winners, this time Newcastle United.

Two shock exits from the Cup in consecutive years had damaged Blackpool's reputation as a great FA Cup side. Indeed, days out at Wembley would not be featuring in the supporters' plans for many years hence, and then it would be play-off matches to get out of divisions the fans in the 1950s must hardly have been aware existed. The side had not, though, become a bad one overnight. There would still be League success and the faithful would not have long to wait. The following season would see Blackpool's highest-ever finish in League football.

So Near and Yet So Far

AFTER their FA Cup triumph three seasons before, A. Brook Hirst, the FA Chairman, had told the Blackpool players that they would be acclaimed all over the country if they won the League championship. It was not just the presence of Stanley Matthews that gave the side its appeal, but a team packed with internationals played attractive and open football that made them one of the most popular visitors at League grounds around the country. The 1955-56 campaign is when they came closest to gaining the reward their football deserved, although by the end Manchester United were clear winners of the title.

Hugh Kelly, for one, believes it would have been the perfect reward for the great Blackpool team of the 1950s who managed to remain a force with changing personnel. He was one player who was there all through the glory years and he admits he loved every minute of it. "Winning the championship would have been something else and as runners-up you can always look back and think of points lost here or there. Yet I loved every minute of my time at Blackpool and although a championship winners' medal would have been wonderful, it was not to be. We still played some terrific football and brought a lot of pleasure to people."

His view is echoed by Allan Brown who says: "At the start of each season in the 1950s there was a feeling we could win the League and this would be the year. We were always hoping. This was the year when we came closest and coining the old football cliché, we just

Blackpool – and arguably football's – most famous player ever, Stanley Matthews pictured on the occasion of his 600th Football League game, for the Seasiders against Newcastle United at Bloomfield Road in November 1959. For Blackpool alone, Sir Stanley, as he later became, made 440 senior appearances.

Blackpool goalkeeper Joe Robinson watches as Manchester United's Charlie Mitten just fails to hook the ball back during

8 FA Cup Final at Wembley. Blackpool lost 4-2 in what has been described as one of the best-ever Wembley Finals.

Harry Johnston leads out the Seasiders in one of his 438 appearances for the club, in a career which began before the war. Johnston, who died when he was only 54, was an influential captain who deserved more than his ten England caps.

Hugh Kelly made 468 appearances for Blackpool and played in both the 1948 and 1951 FA Cup Finals but missed the 1953 Wembley game. He was capped once for Scotland.

Bill Perry (11) sits it out on this occasion during the 1951 FA Cup Final against Newcastle United. Stan Mortensen also looks on as Jack Fairbrother grasps the ball. Blackpool lost 2-0 and another Wembley disappointment had to be borne.

Third time lucky? Stanley Matthews shakes hands with the Duke of Edinburgh before the 1953 FA Cup Final against Bolton Wanderers.

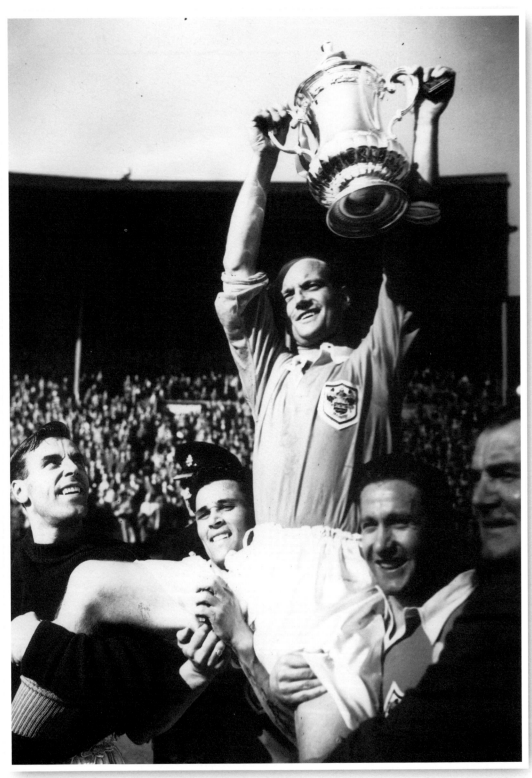

Jubilant Blackpool players hold aloft their skipper Harry Johnston after he received the FA Cup from the Queen. The Seasiders had fought back against Bolton to win a famous Final.

Jackie Mudie, winner of 17 Scottish caps and holder of a remarkable scoring record – 155 goals in 356 games for Blackpool.

An even more prolific goalscorer – Stan Mortensen who netted 222 in 354 games for Blackpool including a hat-trick in the 1953 FA Cup Final.

Just right for Christmas? Stan Mortensen pictured in his Blackpool sports shop in December 1955.

Bolton's Tommy Banks can't stop Stan Matthews at Burnden Park in August 1954. A crowd of over 47,000 saw Bolton win 3-0, though.

South African-born Bill Perry won three
England caps while with Blackpool. Between
1949-50 and 1961-62, Perry scored 129 goals in
436 games for the Seasiders.

Roy Gratrix made 436 senior appearances – and
never scored a goal – for Blackpool between
1953-54 and 1964-65.

George Farm kept goal for Blackpool on 512 occasions – and even scored a goal for the club. Here, though, he is more concerned by the attentions of Arsenal's Derek Tapscott at Highbury in January 1958. Scottish international Farm played in a record 47 consecutive FA Cup games for Blackpool.

Blackpool staff in August 1954, minus Stan Matthews. Back row (left to right): Armfield, Charnley, J. Kelly, Farm, Martin, Snowden, Hauser, Gratrix, Garrett. Front row: Kaye, Mudie, H. Kelly, Peterson, Perry.

Ray Charnley gets in a shot against Burnley's Adam Blacklaw at Turf Moor in October 1959. A crowd of 26,620 saw Blackpool win 4-1.

Ray Charnley, with 222 goals in 407 appearances, was equal with the great Stanley Mortensen in the goalscoring stakes. Charnley's career spanned 1957-58 to 1967-68.

Jimmy Armfield's 627 senior appearances for the Seasiders is, not surprisingly, a club record. Winner of 43 England caps and voted 'the best right-back in the world' after the 1962 World Cup, Armfield enjoyed little success at club level, although he was the major figure when Blackpool regained their top-flight status in 1969-70.

Stanley Matthews and Jackie Mudie, together with Blackburn and England star Ronnie Clayton, pictured on a visit to Thwaites, the Blackburn brewery.

Stanley Matthews pictured after receiving the CBE in January 1956.

Debutant Tony Waiters holds the ball as Blackburn's Roy Vernon comes in. This Boxing Day match at Bloomfield Road in 1959 saw the Seasiders win 1-0 with a goal from Ray Charnley.

Goalkeeper Tony Waiters made 258 senior appearances for Blackpool between 1959-60 and 1966-67. He also played five times for England.

Dave Durie in action against Burnley in October 1960. Durie scored 93 goals in 330 games for Blackpool between 1953-54 and 1963-64.

Roy Gratrix gets in a tackle on Burnley's Willie Irvine in August 1964. The result was a 2-2 draw.

Former Blackpool star Gordon Milne heads Liverpool's third goal past Tony Waiters at Anfield in February 1966. Blackpool lost 4-1.

Glyn James is beaten by Manchester United's George Best at Old Trafford in September 1970. Over 46,000 saw a 1-1 draw. It was a good result but at the end of the season Blackpool were bottom of Division One and their tumble down the League had begun.

took one game at a time, but as the season progressed and we were up there, the players started thinking, 'We can do it.' We just had to keep going until the end, but it slipped away from us and at the end of the season we were left thinking 'if only'. Considering the good players that we had, we should have won the League during this period. We could have done better with the players we had."

Brown adds that all teams have a slip in form during a season. They cannot always perform at the top of their game week in and week out. It is getting through the bad spells and picking up points when the side is not firing on all cylinders that makes the difference between title winners and those who miss out. Too often he feels things didn't go Blackpool's way when a bit of luck or an individual's skill might have made all the difference when the team as a whole was not at its best.

During their best League year, Blackpool chased Manchester United all the way and the runners-up spot marked the highest position the club has ever attained. The old adage that a successful side can always attract good players certainly held true. Two great servants of the club departed in Harry Johnston and Stan Mortensen. But there were players waiting in the wings to take their places and they did not let down the fans, their team-mates, or the memory of the two great players they had replaced. Johnston became manager of Reading, while Morty moved to Hull City in the autumn. Their places were taken by Roy Gratrix and Jackie Mudie respectively.

Gratrix played more than 400 times for Blackpool and was one of the unsung heroes of the side. Many felt the centre-half was unlucky not to play for England and that view was held not just within the town. He was playing for a works team in his native Salford when he was signed by the club. He first made his debut in 1954 at right-back in place of Eddie Shimwell, but when Johnston left Bloomfield Road he switched to centre-half and there he remained until his own departure in the 1964-65 season when he signed for Manchester City, but he made only 15 League appearances before retiring. If the late 1940s and early years of the 1950s had seen a formidable half-back line in Johnston, Hayward and Farrow, it was now matched by Gratrix and the two Kellys – Hugh and Jimmy.

After the débâcle of the previous season, this was more the sort of form the fans wanted to see. The previous year it had been September 25 and the tenth match of the campaign before the terraces could hail a home win. Now they were cheering after the opening match with an impressive 3-1 win against Arsenal and everyone was hoping this was more the real Blackpool rather than the displays produced the previous year. Happily for the nearly 31,000 packed into Bloomfield Road, this game was not a false dawn. The Gunners had taken the lead in the sixth minute. A well-taken strike by Ernie Taylor brought the sides level and gave the Blackpool players a sense of self belief. With Stanley Matthews providing an excellent service to forwards who had suddenly gained the confidence to shoot, there were goals for Bill Perry and Stan Mortensen.

Peter Collins recalls: "Going to watch the games we never thought we would lose because we had such a great side. It is amazing that we only ever finished runners-up and never actually won the title. I guess it is a bit of an indictment of the team really. Wolves were a top side at the time and we beat them home and away that season. We put six past Villa in a terrific game when the players really performed to their best. Sometimes when they hit form, I stood on the terraces and thought they could beat anybody. There were a few big wins and there were huge attendances. It was the best football I saw Blackpool play throughout the season and if we hadn't slipped at the end we might have won it. One win in the last seven games was not championship form."

The confidence in front of goal manifested itself to a thrilling extent on September 3 when Sunderland were the visitors. Manager Joe Smith had warned that one day his players would not only get the ball in front of goal they would shoot while they were there and some team was going to be on the receiving end. It was to be the North East side who conceded seven goals, which included a hat-tick for Bill Perry and two each for Jackie Mudie and Mortensen. It brought Perry's tally to nine in the opening five games of the season. In their defence, Sunderland were reduced to ten men and a limping full-back, but even before that Taylor and Mudie had enjoyed their afternoon at the expense of the defenders. It was the visitors who scored the opening goal against the run of play, but it spurred Blackpool to greater efforts and two goals within three and a half minutes was the response. Sunderland scored three goals by way of consolation but given the Seasiders hit the post three times and missed some other glaring opportunities it could have been far more than seven. This was certainly the form of a championship contender.

A fortnight later, Wolves were the visitors and the game produced a record crowd for Bloomfield Road with over 38,000 squeeing in to see the Seasiders win 2-1.

Ray Hall was due to play for the 'A' side, but a player on National Service had arrived back on leave and was given the chance ahead of him. As someone who preferred playing to watching, he was disappointed, but armed with his player's pass he decided to go to Bloomfield Road and watch the game there.

He recalls: "When I got off the bus, everybody was walking towards me and a chap said the gates had been closed and I was wasting my time. People were milling around looking for a gate that was open. It was awesome. I showed my pass at the players' entrance and somebody shouted: 'They are letting them in here,' and with that there was a stampede for the entrance. The guy on the gate must have thought thousands were going to force their way in. I just managed to squeeze through and we forced the gate shut behind me. Inside they were packed in so tight you couldn't get a cigarette paper between them. I watched the game from the entrance to the players' tunnel and the noise was incredible. It was inspiring. Both Morty and Matthews scored and I felt this was a team at the top." In fact it was Mortensen's final goal for Blackpool.

Yet the great side that had emerged in the early half of the decade was now starting to break up and it was fitting that there was such a large audience to see another of the veterans who had given great service to the club give way to a player who would in time himself become a legend in the coastal resort. After playing in three Cup Finals and being a rock in defence, Eddie Shimwell dislocated a shoulder, which meant he had to hand over his number-two shirt to Jimmy Armfield and would never win it back. The veteran full-back would make one more appearance the following season, at left-back in a 2-1 home defeat by Sunderland, but this was how the packed throng on the terraces would prefer to remember him.

Peter Collins remembers: "When people look back at the Blackpool team of the 1950s it is the forwards everybody remembers and they were great players, but we had some terrific players in defence as well and Eddie Shimwell was as reliable as any of them. If people are asked to remember the players who appeared in all the Finals in this era he is the name that people tend to forget, yet he was a very steady full-back who went about his job without any fuss and he doesn't really get the praise he deserved."

Shimwell had joined the Seasiders in December 1946 from Sheffield United, with Blackpool paying £7,000 for his services. Curiously, he wanted to leave the Yorkshire club because they had refused him permission to run a pub. Sheffield's loss was the Seasiders gain as the full-back played in all three Cup Finals and made 324 League and Cup games for the club in total. He was a robust player with the sliding tackle a speciality. His injury effectively ended his Bloomfield Road career and in May 1957 he went on a free transfer to Oldham Athletic. When his playing career ended, he finally got that pub and became a licensee in Matlock, Derbyshire.

The following month Blackpool suffered a serious reverse and it was to prove a great talking point in the town. Not just because the victors were Preston North End. Nor because the result was a hefty 6-2 defeat. Rather it was because of an injury to goalkeeper George Farm that saw the Scot sent upfield as a centre-forward, only to score one of the goals, a feat he was quick to remind the full-time forwards about. Unfortunately for the Seasiders, the young Armfield did not prove such a success in his role between the posts, although in fairness the side were 2-0 down when he pulled the green jersey on as Preston profited from Farm's shoulder injury, which restricted his movements.

Peter Collins remembers the incident for two reasons. The first was the novelty of seeing the goalkeeper in the centre-forward role and then scoring a goal after having been off for a few minutes for treatment to his shoulder. He was brought back because in the days before substitutes it was thought he might have a nuisance value up front. The second reason, though, was because of the way it showed an attitude to players far removed from the modern game. As he says, why did Blackpool risk aggravating an injury to one of the country's leading goalkeepers in a title-chasing season in a game that was ultimately lost so convincingly anyway? It highlights how the welfare of players did not have the same priority it has today and that could have cost both club and player dearly.

In the Cup, Blackpool travelled to Maine Road to face Manchester City and had the perfect start with Ernie Taylor scoring after only 13 seconds. Unfortunately, fog forced the game to be abandoned and when the match was staged a second time there was to be no such good fortune. Blackpool lost 2-1 and, in the great tradition of football, fans now consoled themselves that they could concentrate on the League. Certainly, there were no hangovers from their Cup appearance when in their next match Aston Villa were the visitors.

It took only five minutes for the first goal and the scoreboard was to be kept ticking over happily as Blackpool finished with six without a Villa reply. An Allan Brown free-kick found defenders flat-footed and Mudie headed the first. By the 20th minute the home side were three goals to the good; Stanley Matthews managed to score his first goal for four months and there were two penalties for Brown. Perry also got in on the act. Serious question marks about the Villa defence there may have been, but it was still an impressive display from Blackpool. The only sour note was that the performance was before what would prove the smallest attendance of the season, only 15,844.

With four matches remaining, Blackpool travelled to League leaders Manchester United for the crunch game of the season. Such was the interest the game generated it produced a then record attendance for Old Trafford of 62,277. If United won they would be champions and they had travelled to an out-of-town training camp to prepare.

Hugh Kelly recalls: "We were looking forward to the game and were confident. You have to approach such games in a positive state of mind. United had not been beaten at home all season but we thought if anybody could do it, than it would be us."

It was not to be against a young Manchester United side that oozed confidence and showed they could battle it out as well as produce some sublime football. An early strike for Dave Durie was not enough for Blackpool. Goals for Johnny Berry, from the penalty spot, and Tommy Taylor were enough to see the side lift the title. For the fans there was plenty to debate on the way home. The decision to penalise George Farm for a challenge on John Doherty appeared harsh and Perry had a strong appeal for a spot-kick turned down when his legs were taken away from him. Yet few could have complained about the final result, with United always looking more dangerous in attack and their defenders more composed.

Hugh Kelly recalls it was the Manchester United team that would be decimated in the Munich air crash within two years. The disaster robbed the game of some outstanding talent. "The Busby Babes were all coming through. It was the first time I had seen Duncan Edwards. I had the ball in our own half, right down in the corner. I had just reached it when this whirlwind arrived and it was Edwards. I thought 'What the heck' and that was my first introduction to him and some of the other young up-and-coming United players. Sadly, in the case of Edwards and many of the others they weren't around long enough for me to get better acquainted with them and their style of play."

Yet before the game he remembers thinking that they could beat United and feeling that, on paper, Blackpool had the better team. He is convinced if the game had been won, the Seasiders would have gone on to win the championship. Earlier in the season, though, he felt the title had slipped away from them. Too many points had had been lost in games that were close and could have produced a Blackpool win. Manchester United had also managed to secure a goalless draw at Bloomfield Road when a home win would have been valuable. The end of Mortensen and Johnston had certainly been factors, but he thought there was still a chance before the Old Trafford defeat.

After their exertions during the season, and with the title lost, the close to the 1955-56 campaign proved a disappointment with three more defeats to end their programme. For a while there was a fear that the runners-up spot might be lost to Wolves, but in the end that proved unfounded as the Seasiders hung on. However, it was not the rousing end to a glorious season that everybody would have liked. It was still, though, the high-water mark in the club's history in League football and to date still is.

Still a Power in the Land

I N THE three seasons that marked the end of the decade, Blackpool showed they were still a team to fear and still a club who could guarantee bumper attendances wherever they played. There were to be no trophies to show for their endeavours, but the town could have had no greater public relations coup than the exploits of its football team. While nowadays the coastal resort is synonymous with tourism, in the 1950s people were as likely to be talking about the football team as the Tower and the Golden Mile.

In the campaigns from 1956 to 1959 they finished fourth, seventh and eighth in the top flight. These were heady times indeed. Jackie Mudie showed he could fill the breech left by the departure of Stan Mortensen and collected 32 goals in the 1956-57 season with another newcomer, Dave Durie, scoring 20. A problem, though, was that while Blackpool were a wonderful draw on their travels, the paying public in the town itself were less enamoured as football had to compete with other attractions. Only four games at Bloomfield Road attracted over 30,000 fans. A local newspaper claimed the town did not deserve First Division football given the paucity of support.

Yet Syd Bevers believes that there was already a feeling that the club had begun the slow decline. Having been to Wembley three times in five years, there was a belief among the supporters that they would always be at the glittering peak of the game. That, of course, wasn't to materialise and as the decade wore on, while still a force he feels the team were not what they were. Mirroring the dip in fortunes was the Atomic Boys' own role at Bloomfield Road.

He explained: "The crowds were starting to fall and many of the players from the Cup Final sides were moving on and I suppose the novelty of the Atomic Boys started to wear off. A lot of genuine supporters want to see good football, but there are many others who are only interested in a winning team. We had brought a bit of colour and a lot of fun to Bloomfield Road and on away matches and we started in the 1940s, so it was time to bring the whole Atomic Boys episode to a close. I still get Christmas cards from many of the players from that era, including Puskas, who the duck was named after."

Bevers adds: "In the late 1950s we could have done more but we kept going along with the old team for a while. We paddled along without making any changes. Blackpool were never a wealthy club and there wasn't as big a transfer market as there is today, but I think we should have been out buying one or two players while we were still near the top. That might have made the difference between being in the top half of the table and actually winning something."

The 1956-57 season marked the end of Allan Brown's Blackpool career, much to the disappointment of the player himself. This was a time when clubs had proprietorial control over players and what they said went. The fact that Brown had no wish to leave Bloomfield Road was of no consequence. It is a fact that still rankles with the former Scottish international who had served the club so well. The decision to sell him to Luton Town would rebound on the club and have an unforeseen benefit for the player. That, though, was to come later.

Remembering his departure he said: "It was Joe Smith who wanted to sell me but I was happy here. He had Dave Durie to take my place so he decided to get a bit of cash. As a player I had no say in the matter. I was just called in and told that everything was sorted. Joe Smith knew as much about being a football manager as he did about being a farmer. He wasn't a manager in the modern style at all."

Blackpool's fourth place was earned thanks to a superb end to the season. They lost only three of their last 15 games and a winning sequence that lasted eight games was started with a comprehensive win against relegation-haunted Charlton Athletic at The Valley. Stan Matthews and Ernie Taylor were at their best against a defence that was not up to the task. Playing out on the flanks avoided the worst of the thick mud that was always likely to be a more formidable obstacle to the Blackpool attack than anybody in a Charlton shirt. The final score was 4-0 with Mudie collecting two and Brown a third, in his last match, while Blackpool's opening goal came courtesy of a Derek Ufton own-goal.

Buoyed by this success, Blackpool enjoyed victory over both Manchester clubs in their next two games. They beat Manchester City 4-1, which would have helped ruin the day out for the Mancunians who made the trip to Blackpool, and then the Seasiders travelled to Old Trafford and recorded an impressive 2-0 win over the side who would win the title, with Bill Perry and Dave Durie collecting the goals.

A Boxing Day encounter with Leeds United at Elland Road gave the Atomic Boys one of their last outings and the chance to defy the ban on Puskas the duck. Their own bird had been left in Blackpool due to an outbreak of fowl pest that was one of the main reasons for the non-appearance of Puskas in the 1950s. The Ministry of Agriculture and Fisheries placed a ban on the movement of fowl and there was no exception, not even for the Seasiders' mascot. Yet when they arrived at their hotel somebody came in with a duck. The man dressed as an ATS girl agreed to smuggle it in and release it in the centre-circle. The whole procedure went like clockwork except it was impossible to grab the duck and make an escape before officials arrived.

Bevers takes up the story: "After the game I went to collect the duck and a police inspector told me I wasn't allowed to put a duck on the pitch. I told him it wasn't me, which was true, and that I had just come to collect it. He sent a constable to go and get the bird, but unfortunately it had escaped and got under the stand. The constable had a hell of a job trying to catch it and all we could hear was him cursing the duck as he tried to grab it, but it kept getting away. When he emerged he was covered from head to toe in dust and clutching the duck. He wasn't happy but then neither were we. Leeds won 5-0 that day so the duck didn't bring us too much luck."

In the FA Cup, Blackpool's opening fixture was a difficult trip to Burnden Park. The following year Bolton Wanderers would make it all the way to Wembley, but in this campaign they would fail at the first hurdle as the Seasiders had the measure of them in a close-fought game that ended with a 3-2 victory. It brought a home fixture against Second Division Fulham and the Londoners were demolished in a 6-2 rout in which Mudie scored four goals with a Derek Lampe own-goal and one for Durie completing the demolition.

The fifth-round draw produced First Division opposition in the shape of West Bromwich Albion. Blackpool turned in a performance well below par at Bloomfield Road and the match ended without a goal scored. For the replay, more than 1,000 Blackpool fans made the journey and they were confident that the side would play truer to form for this match. There was a double incentive: a sixth-round tie against Arsenal and the chance for the England contingent in their ranks to impress the watching international selectors.

The visiting fans could not have asked for a better start with a goal after two minutes. The build-up was classic Blackpool. Ernie Taylor combined with Stan Matthews. The winger dribbled to the edge of the box and then crossed to the unmarked Bill Perry who shot into the bottom left-hand corner of the net. After seven minutes it should have been two, but a Durie strike was disallowed for offside. The visiting fans were convinced it was the wrong decision and it would prove costly for their side. Having dominated for the first 20 minutes, Blackpool now ceded control to the Albion and were made to pay. When Farm failed to hold a lob while being challenged the ball was worked back to Ronnie Allen who scored the equaliser. In the second half the defence held out until with eight minutes to go Derek Kevan scored the winner to end Blackpool's interest in the FA Cup for another year.

The slow decline in Blackpool's fortunes continued in the 1957-58 campaign when the side managed seventh place without ever really challenging. No player scored more than 20 goals – although that would still be a fine return today – and the heretical view was being heard on the terraces that perhaps age was starting to take its toll on the great Matthews. Rumours were starting to circulate that he would be going back to Stoke City, but for the moment they were unfounded. The winger remained but another great stalwart of the club departed with Joe Smith succumbing to ill health after 23 years as manager.

A new arrival on the first-team scene was Ray Charnley, who would become Blackpool's most prolific goalscorer behind Jimmy Hampson and Stan Mortensen, and they were a hard act to compete with. He was signed from non-League Morecambe in May 1957, for £1,000, and would be a player who oversaw the club from its glory days into Second Division football. Towards the end of his career he was one of the few saving graces in an increasingly poor team. Charnley was top scorer in seven of the 11 seasons he was at Bloomfield Road and scored his 100th League goal in only his 156th game, a record bettered only by Harry Bedford, a pre-war Blackpool star. In total Charnley scored 222 goals in 407 League and Cup appearances and won one England cap, in 1962 against France. He left in 1967 and joined Preston as part of a change in personnel instigated by the new manager Stan Mortensen.

He said: "When I joined Blackpool I thought I was quite lucky. There were three other centre-forwards at the club and they were probably all ahead of me, but fortunately for me, although not for them, they were all injured and I played in September 1957 against Luton Town. I got a couple of first-team games within weeks of signing in a team that contained virtually all the leading players of the great Blackpool side. There must have been half a dozen of the 1953 Cup-winning side still there and with Stan Matthews and Bill Perry firing over crosses, we could still score a lot of goals. It was still quite a decent side and the club could still attract players before the abolition of the maximum wage."

As well as suddenly playing alongside internationals, Charnley had to quickly get used to the rigours of professional football life with training mornings and afternoons. He noticed the difference when he was allowed to turn out for Morecambe in a match against Lancaster City soon after arriving at Bloomfield Road. With his extra fitness and the higher standard of football he had been exposed to in training, he scored five goals. It proved that the work at Blackpool was making a significant difference. Soon he would be playing regularly in the Blackpool first team.

His game against Luton slipped by, but his real memory is of his first home game, against Sunderland before a full house. "I was nervous, but fortunately I scored an early goal and there is no better way to settle yourself as a centre-forward. The only sad part was I spent half the time in the dressing-room with concussion after a clash of heads. I scored the second when I came back on. When I first started, all I was really thinking about was myself and doing my own job. Where we were in the table never concerned me then, I was just glad to be playing."

Peter Collins was a great fan of the centre-forward saying: "Ray could head a ball better than anybody. He used to get a sort of whiplash affect on the ball that produced tremendous power. He was the leading goalscorer year in and year out and, like so many others, he returned to the town when his playing days were over, and worked as a painter and decorator. Unlike today there was not the money in football that meant players could retire to villas in France or Spain when there playing days were up. They all got jobs or started in business. Ray bridged the gap from the glory days in the late 1950s to relegation and the Second Division and during that time he was a great servant to the club."

The results in the 1957-58 season were a mixed bag, but one match stands out. Sunderland were the visitors to Bloomfield Road on October 5 and they were on the receiving end of a 7-0 mauling. It was comfortably the Seasiders' best result of the season. The goal rush started after only 45 seconds when Durie headed home a corner. Against a struggling defence there were two more goals in the next ten minutes with Durie and Charnley both taking advantage of goalkeeping mistakes. The game was effectively won and the Blackpool players produced an exhibition display to the delight of the crowd. Charnley had his second before the break and there was a huge ovation for the side at half-time. In the second half, Perry was injured and virtually a passenger in the side, but any hopes the visitors might have entertained that they could put a stop to the Seasiders' goalscoring ways were quickly dispelled. The loss of Charnley on the hour with a head injury should have given Sunderland hope but, despite the injuries, two quick goals for Taylor were followed by one for the struggling Perry. It marked Blackpool's biggest-ever home victory in the Football League and matched the 7-0 against Preston North End at Deepdale in 1948.

Blackpool's hopes in the Cup did not get past the third round when they suffered their heaviest post-war defeat in the competition against Second Division West Ham United. Although it was a huge disappointment, the thousand or so Blackpool supporters who made the journey could point to the absence of internationals Ernie Taylor and Jackie Mudie through injury that had undermined the side's cause and blunted its attacking potential. Bill Perry passed a fitness test only on the morning of the match. The West Ham team had also been enjoying a good run of form, taking 31 points from 25 games and only having been beaten once at home.

Preparations put in place at Bloomfield Road for a replay proved unduly optimistic as Blackpool found themselves outplayed. Yet it was the visitors who had the best possible start with a second-minute penalty converted by Hugh Kelly. The Blackpool net came under intense pressure, but when a goal did arrive it was due to an error by the normally immaculate Jimmy Armfield whose clearance fell invitingly for Vic Keeble. The player would collect a hat-trick and there were two goals for Johnny Dick in a comprehensive victory.

At the end of the season it was clear that football was still a profitable business at this time. With the maximum wage still in place, overheads were kept low and although the crowds were slipping from the great days of the late 1940s and early 1950s, a stake in a football club was not the financial nightmare it so often is nowadays with barely a handful of the League clubs making a profit. Blackpool announced a profit of £9,335 on the 1957-58 season compared to £6,199 the previous year. Gate receipts and the club's quota of away match receipts totalled £86,921, which was £9,306 down on the figure for 1956-57. Other figures revealed in the accounts were wages, bonuses and benefits totalled £31,000; training and travelling £12,201; and ground expenses were £16,549.

In 1958-59, the Seasiders, under the guidance of new manager Ron Suart, slipped one place, finishing eighth in the League. Charnley proved the leading goalscorer with 20. It was a promising early start to the campaign in which the first three games were won. The Seasiders travelled to White Hart Lane for the opening match of the season and there triumphed 3-2. This was followed with home victories over Newcastle United and Manchester United. However, their League form was never consistent enough to realistically challenge. The best result was a 5-0 victory over Chelsea in March in which Perry and Mudie both scored two and there was one for Charnley. The season saw the opening of floodlights at Bloomfield Road for the first time. The first match played under lights was a friendly against the Scottish League champions Hearts on Monday, October 13.

In the FA Cup, Blackpool reached the sixth round. They had travelled to Southampton and achieved a 2-1 win at The Dell. The fourth round saw them again on their travels this time visiting Ashton Gate where Bristol City were the opponents. A 1-1 result was enough for a return to Bloomfield Road and a Durie goal settled the issue. For the next round, West Bromwich Albion were the visitors and although they were First Division opposition they proved no match for the Seasiders, succumbing 3-1. The sixth round produced a tie with another First Division side, Luton Town, and the return of an old favourite, Allan Brown.

The former Blackpool player played a key role in helping earn a draw and set up a replay at Luton. Bill Perry was missing for the match at Kenilworth Road in which history was not with the visitors, who had won only one of their four post-war visits to the ground. Such was the excitement in the town, with Wembley only two games away, that the 30,069 attendance established a new record for the club beating the 28,433 who watched when Luton played Arsenal, also in a sixth-round tie in 1952. For Brown it was not the best overall performance he had produced but he scored the only goal of the game to send the Hatters through to the semi-finals. Luton would go all the way to Wembley, only to be beaten by ten-man Nottingham Forest in the Final. Blackpool created plenty of goalscoring opportunities, but were unable to convert any, and in the Cup you only get one chance.

Brown said: "We worked hard to get a draw at Bloomfield Road and then it was a big day for Luton when they came down. It was a close game and it fell to me to settle it. I had the job of pushing one past George Farm. I put it through his legs to win the game. It was a bit of a blow. George used to be my room-mate whenever we went away. I still see George and remind him about that goal. He's just the same. He always kept himself fit and he is still a fit man. I hadn't wanted to go to Luton but that year we went to Wembley so after twice missing out with Blackpool I finally got a chance to play there in the Cup Final although we lost to Nottingham Forest. It was curious the way it worked out. Particularly with knocking out Blackpool on the way."

Hugh Kelly remembers that one of the perks enjoyed by the players in this era was the pre-season tour abroad. His most memorable came in 1958 when the team set off on a six-week tour that took in America, Fiji, Honolulu and Australia before finishing with two games in Hong Kong. It was in Hong Kong, where the side were due to play a local XI, that he remembers the British Ambassador had joked they would face a difficult game and a Chinese delegation had walked out. "Afterwards we learnt they thought the ambassador had not shown us sufficient respect and had slighted us. On the night it didn't matter as their famous local side were beaten 10-1. We always had good trips but that was special. We stayed at top hotels and saw the sights."

In Australia there were many locals who had emigrated and they remembered the team and the players. People would ask questions about the three FA Cup Finals. With the players on the maximum wage such jaunts were a nice bonus. The fame of the club and Stanley Matthews meant they were always in great demand. As Kelly says: "While everybody else was travelling to Blackpool for their holidays, we were setting off all over the world. I suppose the club must have received good money to take us on tour but we didn't know that at the time. The hospitality was terrific. They were wonderful times."

Joe Smith and the Managers

I N THE mid-1930s, Blackpool were a Second Division side whose brief three-season taste of the top division had ended in 1932-33, when they finished bottom after narrowly escaping relegation the previous two years. Although they had a long history, there was little glory along the way. Those three years were their only time in the top flight. That was to change and much of the credit can be laid at the door of one man. Joe Smith was charged with changing their fortunes and it was his vision and expertise that laid the foundations for the most successful period in the club's history, which saw them reach the very heights of the game. He was in charge at Bloomfield Road for 23 years and was Blackpool's greatest manager.

He arrived with an enviable playing record that commanded respect as soon as he joined in 1935. As an inside-left for Bolton Wanderers, his goalscoring prowess would be eclipsed only by the iconic Nat Lofthouse. In his 15 seasons with the club, he scored 277 goals in 492 appearances and appeared in Wanderers' victorious 1923 and 1926 Cup Finals. He had the honour of being the first captain to lift the trophy at Wembley Stadium. It was a career that began in April 1909, in a 2-0 defeat at West Bromwich Albion, and would see four seasons lost due to World War One. His last game for the club was in a 2-1 victory over Liverpool at Burnden Park on New Year's Day 1927. He represented England five times, a figure that would have been higher but for the war. From Bolton he joined

Stockport County where he scored 61 goals in 69 League games and had spells with Darwen and Manchester Central before going into management.

His first taste of management was at Reading, where he was in charge for four years. He quickly showed he could make the transition, twice achieving a runners-up position for the Third Division South side. It was said that a love of the seaside was one of the reasons for taking up the appointment at Blackpool. Whatever the reason, the signing of Smith was to prove a masterstroke.

Smith's task was helped in that he replaced a manager in Alex 'Sandy' McFarlane who was unpopular with the players and rumours of dressing-room discontent were rife. However, his predecessor had overhauled the playing side and his last season had seen the club in fourth place in the Second Division. Now Smith would establish Blackpool as one of the most popular teams in the country in the post-war years. Within two seasons the Seasiders had won promotion and the club was on its path to glory.

Hugh Kelly remembers Smith as a wonderful man who had no enemies. He points out, though, that the role of the manager in the post-war years was far different to the job today. There was not the emphasis on tactics and planning. The manager was never seen on the training field in a tracksuit, but rather had a largely administrative role. However, the player recalls that what Smith did say was worth listening to. He remembers the first time some of the senior players decided on a tactical plan.

He said: "We were playing Chelsea and we had heard all about Jimmy Greaves. He was being hailed down south as a wonder boy and in those days any northern team used to play that bit extra when we played the southern teams, particularly if they were boasting about a brilliant new player. The lads just wanted to go down and get at them. Shortly before the kick-off, a few senior players gathered in the corner and decided we should single out Greaves for special marking. Really clamp on him and see what happened. There was a newspaper on the table extolling the virtues of the young Greaves.

"Joe walked in and all he said was that we were on the six o'clock train back so we had better be quick with the bath and getting changed. He saw us in the corner and asked what was happening and he was told the idea of man-marking Greaves. He screwed up the newspaper with an article on the talents of Greaves and threw it in the bin, telling us: 'Just go out and play your own game,' which we did and had a good win. That was the end of the first tactical planning meeting we had ever had."

He adds: "Joe never did much talking because he thought he had the best bunch of lads in the League and he trusted us to go out and do our best. He was a fatherly figure. He would walk along the touchline and see how we were progressing during training, but he didn't take part in any coaching. We just all fitted in with each other. As far as day-to-day dealings went, we never really had any with Joe. Also, the team never changed much for years unless there was an injury. It would be the same names on the team sheet for week after week and season after season. The team picked itself."

Even so, he believes that Smith did not get the recognition he deserved from the football world at large, for the work he did at Blackpool. Certainly the southern clubs used to get the lion's share of any publicity that was going until first Manchester United and then Liverpool put an end to the southern bias. For the manager of a small-town club in the north of England, it was hard to get the press interest both he and his team deserved.

The hands-off approach certainly suited Stanley Matthews. It would, though, have been a brave manager who tried to dictate to the great man how he should play. Matthews always believed Smith had the right idea in trusting his players to play their own game and knowing that they wouldn't give up. An example he often cited was during half-time in the 1951 Cup Final when it had been a poor opening half and neither team were at their best. All Smith did was put it down to nerves and encouraged his players to show more confidence in their own ability. There was no rollicking for the first-half display. Nor was there an attempt by the manager to lay down tactics to the team. All he did was encourage and show he had faith in his players.

Yet Allan Brown is less of a fan of the manager, even though he recognises he was an outstanding player for Bolton Wanderers during his day. He feels his talents working with the players were limited. Certainly in the administrative side of the club Smith took business decisions regardless of the feelings of players. In Brown's case that included selling him to Luton Town for around £10,000 when he didn't want to go. Yet in many respects Blackpool were no different from any other club in their treatment of players. The status of professional footballers generally was low and the clout they could bring to bear virtually non-existent.

The player confirms that Smith was not a master tactician. There were no team talks from him and he didn't get involved in coaching or training. Brown recalls: "The limit of his pre-match advice would be things like 'Give the ball to Stan [Matthews] at every opportunity,' and that would be it. I remember we always used to come in on a Tuesday after having Monday as a rest day. We always had a full-scale practice match with the Reserves and they always beat us. Joe would be up in the stand shouting his head off. Once Ernie Taylor was working his way into the penalty box and when he got to the penalty-spot Joe shouted: 'Hit it, hit it!' and Ernie stopped, turned round and told him where to go in no uncertain terms. The Reserves were playing full out and we were going through the motions, but whatever happened on the Tuesday they never put reserves in on the Saturday. We were still getting over the weekend's match and they were keener."

He adds: "Joe was a character, but he didn't get too involved in the football. I remember once playing Cardiff City and we were winning at half-time and in walks Joe. We looked up, expected to hear a few words about the game, and all he told us was that we had to hurry up at the end because the coach was going to be away in 15 minutes. He wasn't too worried about Cardiff. All he wanted was to get the coach away and beat the crowd."

Peter Collins understands from working at the club, and talking to players who served under Smith, that the manager saw his role as collecting the best players for the different positions and selling those who were surplus to requirements or for whom age was catching up. Once he had the team he wanted, he didn't coach them. Rather he left them to go out and do their best. Hopefully they would succeed in bringing results and justify his decision to buy them. He expected them to know what they had to do.

Yet as Collins explains, football was very different then and was far more regimented. The winger stayed on the wing, the full-back marked him, the centre-half shadowed the centre-forward, etc. There were not the tactics and the different formations there are today. The structure of the game was well defined and predictable. The way Smith operated as manager was no different to the vast majority of clubs in the League.

Bill Perry said: "Everybody adapts to the situation at the time. In our days we had no coach, rarely had team talks or discussions about the order of play. It was not just at Blackpool, but that was pretty much the same everywhere. Joe was of the old school and he felt if a player was good enough for the first team, then he was good enough to think for himself on the field and make decisions in split seconds as they happened. If they couldn't do that, then in his eyes they were not good enough for the first team at Blackpool.

"His strength was in knowing which players to pick for certain positions to complement the team he had. He could put a player into the position where his talents, as Joe saw them, would be best utilised, but once he was there it was up to the individual to think for himself. Joe would not dictate how anybody should play. Situations developed on the field and, in his view, they can't be coached, other than set-pieces like throw-ins, corners and free-kicks. That was the philosophy of Joe Smith."

Although he had disagreements over money with the club, Jock Dodds says simply: "He was one of the best managers ever, alongside the greats. His record proves that. He knew the players to buy and those to transfer and that was his great skill. His team talks were legendary. He once gathered us round before a game and told someone to shut the door so he wouldn't be overheard. Then he told us: 'The man with the biggest heart wins.' And that was it. If he got excited, you had to watch out because he would throw his arms about."

Another anecdote he recalls concerned a Scottish player who had come down for a trial and was given a game in the Reserves when the second-team matches could attract a sizeable crowd. Smith called the player over and said: "When you go out, do your best. Now whatever the result, I want you to come off the field last." When the player asked why, he was told by Smith he wanted to gauge the crowd's reaction to the newcomer. The game went badly, Blackpool lost heavily, and the fans made their feelings felt. Smith invited the lad into his office: "Did you hear all the booing?" he asked. The player said he had but that there was some cheering as well. To which Smith replied: "That wasn't for you. They were showing their appreciation of the booing."

Dodds recalls on his arrival from Sheffield United, a factor had been the weather and the standard of living. An industrial city like Sheffield was not as pleasant to live in as Blackpool and Smith was well aware of the attraction of the place. He told Dodds: "It is worth £10 a week extra to play in Blackpool because of the weather and the lifestyle."

One of the last of Joe Smith's signings was Ray Charnley and his memory of Smith is that he was simply a legend. He said: "He whipped up enthusiasm. He used to watch practice matches and shout obscene comments at the players when they made mistakes. He never came down on to the pitch to show us how it should be done. I never saw him in a tracksuit. He was the driving force behind the success, though, and everything started to slide after he left."

The shadow of Joe Smith falls across all that was best about Blackpool in their glory years. Finding a successor when ill health forced his retirement in 1958 was never going to be easy. For whoever followed it proved less a picking up of the baton from a man who had enjoyed 21 of his 23 managerial years in the First Division, and had never been out of the top flight since the war, than being handed a poisoned chalice. Former Blackpool player Ron Suart was the man given the thankless task.

Suart had joined Blackpool in 1938 but war intervened before he could graduate to the first team and it was with the resumption of the League in 1946 that the full-back got his chance. In 1948 he suffered the blow of playing in all the rounds of the FA Cup, only to miss out on the Final due to injury, and many believe his defensive skills were missed on the day. In his fourth season at the club he went on the transfer list, unable to command a regular first-team place. He was signed by Blackburn Rovers for £12,000 and spent six seasons at Ewood Park.

His apprenticeship in management was first served as player-manager of non-League Wigan Athletic before he took the manager's job at Scunthorpe United. His appointment at Blackpool was well received and given the club were now beginning the start of their long, slow decline, he did all he could to halt the process. He was particularly adept at spotting young talent and signed Alan Ball and Graham Rowe. The harsh economics of football in the 1960s, with the maximum wage gone, were to make his job very difficult and the peaks which the club had enjoyed in the 1950s were never going to be scaled again.

Too often the fans and the press rounded on him for failings in the club that he could do little about. The reality of 1960s football was that small provincial towns were increasingly struggling to compete with the big city clubs. The fate of Blackpool was being shared by other East Lancashire clubs like Bolton, Preston, Blackburn and Burnley. Yet for a town weaned on success in the 1950s, the finger of blame had to be pointed somewhere and it was in many ways unfairly levelled at the quietly-spoken Suart.

The baying of the mob calling for his head began as early as the 1960-61 season, where Blackpool flirted with relegation and suffered a humiliating 6-2 defeat against Second Division Scunthorpe United in the third round of the FA Cup. He survived that call for his resignation and then helped the Seasiders to limp along in the bottom half of the top flight until 1966-67, when the end finally came. Some might argue that without his talents the First Division trapdoor may well have swung open far earlier. His critics believe he didn't do enough to bring about the changes that would have helped keep Blackpool in the top flight.

There was a lot of interference from the board in team selection and transfers. But that was not unusual at this time. Tommy Banks, the Bolton Wanderers and England full-back, recalls directors at Burnden Park sending half-time advice to internationals on tactics when their experience extended to no more than Sunday League football. If results were going badly for a side, the more directors who were *au fait* with business, but fairly clueless in football, would be anxious to get involved. Before the relegation denouement, Suart fell on his sword, offering his resignation in January 1967. It was accepted. He later served at Chelsea as assistant manager to Tommy Docherty and Dave Sexton, and briefly held the manager's post in 1974. The respect he had earned as a player was never lost throughout his career in management.

Perry recalls there was a change of emphasis when Suart arrived. He was full of the new ideas of the day and had studied as an FA coach. The era of hands-on coaching was beginning and Suart was in the forefront. It was all a far cry from the days of Joe Smith. Now instead of players being left to do their own thing on the field and read the game as it unfolded, the squad were taught set plays and tactics. Unfortunately, Perry believes, in many cases he was trying to get players to do things they were not capable of carrying out. They were roles alien to them. Players had never before had to attempt to fit into rigid game plans.

He said: "I was 28 years old and I was being asked to do things I'd never tried before and wasn't capable of doing. I told him: 'Look Ron, it is all right talking to a young kid of 18 to 20 about something like this because they are at an age where they can adapt, but I'm too long in the teeth to change my style.' That was where both Ron and Blackpool went wrong. The seeds had been sown, but it was shortly after I left that the decline became apparent at Blackpool."

Ray Charnley was also less enamoured of the new manager, who he had played against in his Morecambe days when Suart was turning out for Wigan. He sums up the new boss simply with the words: "He was OK."

If the departure of Joe Smith had heralded the beginning of the end, and the resignation of Ron Suart had come just as the curtain came down on the glory years for Blackpool, there was still time for one of the great Bloomfield Road legends to take his place in the manager's chair. Stan Mortensen was appointed in February 1967, and not surprisingly it was a move welcomed by the fans. There was insufficient time to breath life into a side that won only one game at home all season, and less than four months later Blackpool slipped from the top flight after finishing in bottom place in the First Division. It would be left to Morty to try and resurrect the Seasiders' fortunes in the lower division. He would ultimately fail and although he was building the foundations for a side that might have challenged for promotion, his contract was terminated in April 1969 in a move that both angered and baffled the fans.

A Relegation Battle

THE 1959-60 season saw the gradual decline in Blackpool's fortunes continue as the side finished 11th in the League. Too many of the great players from the side's glory days earlier in the 1950s were now bowing out and the replacements were not able to take the club to the heights they had previously enjoyed. They would never again finish in the top half of the table and a portent for the future would come the following year when the relegation trapdoor so nearly swung open for the Seasiders.

It is useful to look at the basement of the First Division in 1960-61. Blackpool escaped relegation by a single point. Preston North End were bottom. A third of the small-town Lancashire clubs, Bolton Wanderers, were in 18th place. For both Blackpool and Bolton, the death knell had not yet sounded. It would not, though, be long in coming because with the abolition of the maximum wage and dwindling crowds, their days were numbered. For all the Lancashire sides who had known glory in the 1950s, there was to be a long and inexorable fall with just the occasional rally to briefly raise the fans hopes. Preston fell the first and the furthest. Bolton would be the next. Remarkably after coming so close to the relegation zone, Blackpool would struggle on as a perennial basement side. For all the clubs the grind of matches against unfashionable sides in the lower reaches of the Football League would soon begin.

For 1959-60, though, there was still the chance to see echoes of the great years of the early and mid-1950s. Stanley Matthews was still plying his trade on the wing, and in Ray Charnley he had a centre-forward who was maturing into a useful First Division player. Charnley would net 18 times in the season. On the field, the results never looked like being good enough to challenge. The low point was a 6-0 home demolition at the hands of Manchester United, who could easily have scored a few more. Interest in the FA Cup didn't last beyond the fourth round when, having travelled to Ewood Park and gained a respectable 1-1 draw, Blackburn Rovers then won the replay convincingly 3-0 and would go on to reach the Final.

Those departing included Ewan Fenton and George Farm. The successor to the Scottish international in the Blackpool goal was Tony Waiters, who would win international honours for England. Farm's was a hard act to follow, but Waiters did and in many eyes even managed to eclipse his talented predecessor. In the post-war years, Blackpool had enjoyed a succession of fine goalkeepers going back to Jock Wallace who bridged the gap between pre and post-war football. The man who had won England amateur honours would keep the tradition of quality goalkeepers alive, even if the rest of the side was a shadow of the 1950s teams. In the England side he took over from another legend, Gordon Banks, and played five times for his country. He retired in May 1967, while still only 30 to concentrate on coaching.

The following year, one win in the first 13 games of the new campaign brought fears of relegation. That one victory, though, was an impressive 5-3 victory at home to Aston Villa. When they hit form, the forwards could still rattle up some big scores and for a relegation-haunted side they achieved some impressive wins. Later in the campaign they would twice more bag a nap-hand of goals, against both Leicester City and Wolves. It was not, though, to be the biggest win of the season.

After their disastrous opening games, the pessimistic talk on the terraces was eased slightly with three wins in a row, beginning with a 4-0 victory over Nottingham Forest at Bloomfield Road on October 22, and then a superb 2-1 win against the reigning League champions,

Burnley, at Turf Moor. The scene was set for Blackpool's best result of the season when Cardiff City were the visitors. It was reckoned the most impressive performance by the team for a long time and six goals were the reward with Charnley collecting a hat-trick and Ray Parry, Bill Perry and Dave Durie all on target as well. In three games the Seasiders had scored 12, conceded only two and collected all six points. Fans argued that it was not the form of relegation contenders, although worryingly, even in the six-goal romp Stan Matthews had a quiet game. The problem, though, was that such goalfests were all too rare and too many goals were being conceded.

Getting among the goalscorers would not have been unusual for Durie earlier in his career, but towards the end of the previous season Suart had switched the long-serving player from his usual inside-forward position to left-half in a bid to shore up the defence. Durie had begun his Blackpool career in March 1953, in a 1-0 win at Turf Moor, and although first-team chances were hard to come by in his early career, he eventually replaced Allan Brown at inside-forward. In 1956-57 he and Jackie Mudie scored 52 League goals between them. He quickly acclimatised to a defensive role and remained at Bloomfield Road until the 1963-64 season, by which time he had played 330 games for the club.

Charnley recalls: "After the 1950s, this was the season that brought home to us that Blackpool were no longer one of the top teams. The legends who made up the old guard were never properly replaced and although we survived this season, from now on it was a case of always seeming to have to worry about relegation. After this year we knew that unless something drastic was done – and there seemed little chance of that – Blackpool couldn't live with the top city clubs, and the Cup Finals the club had been in suddenly seemed a long time before."

A lot of responsibility was thrust on players who had matured in the club's heyday. Jimmy Armfield was born in Denton, Manchester, but had been raised in Blackpool and was spotted by Joe Smith during a practice match and offered a trial. He played his first game in December 1954, against Portsmouth, and was to stay 17 years. He arrived with memories of the 1953 FA Cup win still fresh and would end his career with a First Division relegation campaign in 1971. It was the second time he had suffered the ignominy of the drop from the top flight with the one club he served throughout this career.

As a long-serving captain for Blackpool, it was often his energy and driving ambition that made the difference between First Division survival and relegation. He was a fast, committed full-back who is famed for developing the overlap that is so much a part of the modern game. He was Young Footballer of the Year in 1959 and was runner-up Footballer of the Year in 1966, edged out by Bobby Charlton. He first appeared for England in 1959, against Brazil, and won a total of 43 caps of which 15 were as captain. He played his last game for Blackpool in May 1971, in a 1-1 draw against Manchester United, and received a testimonial on his 35th birthday. In all, he played 627 games for the club and, as the quality of those around him gradually grew more mediocre, he was increasingly the quality player in the Seasiders' defence.

Ron Suart had become the target of the fans' anger as results up to the three-match winning run had been so disappointing. However, he faced a rebuilding task with yet more key personnel bowing to the inevitable passage of time with Hugh Kelly and Jackie Mudie the most notable. There were also some new arrivals, many of whom were to make their name at Bloomfield Road in the coming years, including Glyn James, a future Welsh international. Yet it was an experienced player snapped up for £25,000 whose arrival had sparked the Blackpool mini-revival. Many believed the purchase of Ray Parry from Bolton Wanderers not only ensured the club's First Division status, but also kept Suart in a job. He took over the inside-forward berth of the great Jackie Mudie, who left for Stoke City for £8,500 in March 1961.

Derby-born Parry (his brother Jack was a great servant of the Rams) was the youngest player to appear in the First Division when he played for Bolton Wanderers against Wolves on October 13, 1951, aged 15 years and 267 days. He was a member of Wanderers' 1958 Cup-winning side and played twice for England. In all, he played one game short of 300 for Bolton and there was disappointment on the Burnden Park terraces that he was allowed to leave. His performances for the Seasiders proved there was still a few good years left and perhaps Bolton were unwise to let him go. He stayed at Bloomfield Road for four years before moving to Bury, where he passed the milestone of 500 League games. He remained in League football until 1972.

The breathing space enjoyed by Suart was not to last and soon the results had a depressing familiarity about them. When League form is faltering, a good Cup run can ignite the passions of the crowd and raise the players' spirits. A visit to Scunthorpe United, though, proved a humiliating experience. Blackpool were humbled 6-2 after having been in the lead 2-1 at the break. As expected when lower division opposition takes on one of the top-flight teams, Scunthorpe battled for everything, were quicker into the tackle, direct going forward and refused to be overawed by their illustrious opponents. The defeat was the biggest for Blackpool in the competition since 1913 when they lost 6-1 at Tottenham. There was to be no better fortune in the newly-inaugurated Football League Cup with Leeds United progressing after a replay at Bloomfield Road. As worrying as the result was the fact that this match was the first time in 15 years that the attendance had slipped below 10,000, with only 9,614 watching.

Correspondents to the *Evening Gazette* who suggested, after the all-too-brief revival, that Blackpool could be collecting the talent money for a top-four finish, were soon proved wildly optimistic. With four League games remaining, the club's First Division future was still in the balance. A home victory against Newcastle United was a welcome return to winning ways after three successive defeats. Next was a visit to Maine Road, where the Seasiders desperately needed at least a point.

Conditions were not conducive to good football with part of the pitch waterlogged while other areas were hard where the ice had not melted. It meant the ball would either stop dead or shoot away quickly. It certainly added to the excitement, especially for the travelling Blackpool fans with so much at stake. Manchester City were in inspired form, thanks to the work of Denis Law. Twice Armfield was forced to clear off the line from the Scottish forward, once heading clear a powerful shot which left him stunned and then again using his head to keep out a well-judged lob. City also hit the bar when goalkeeper Gordon West deflected a shot. Law was on target in the 51st minute after being put clear by Barry Betts and giving West no chance with the shot. Twenty minutes later, a Matthews corner-kick was met by a Bruce Crawford header and Blackpool were level. As the visitors desperately tried to hang on for a point, Law looked to have settled the game with just three minutes remaining when his miscued shot went past West, only for the goalkeeper to slide through the goalmouth mud, stop the ball with one hand, and then do a juggling act with it before seeing it safely round the post.

Victory in the penultimate game away to Birmingham City would ensure the preservation of First Division status and it was duly achieved in a match that was never pretty, but given all that was at stake that was understandable. Team spirit and a never-say-die attitude from every player, from the youngest, 18-year-old Gordon West, to the elder statesman the 46-year-old Stanley Matthews, ensured that on muddy conditions and in heavy rain they played with a ferocity their opponents could not match. Brian Peterson scored the first in the ninth minute when he profited from a mistake by Birmingham goalkeeper Johnny Schofield. Crawford's goal after good work by Peterson and Parry settled the match. A 3-3 draw with Manchester City completed the season. It had been a narrow escape.

Terminal Decline

T HE 1960s brought little cheer, as having just escaped relegation Blackpool now found themselves firmly lodged in the lower half of the table. They would remain in the top division for five seasons before the inevitable drop. What was hard for the fans was that the Seasiders were no longer generating the aura they once had. Rather, each new campaign was a battle for survival and it was often far from pretty to watch.

On the terraces the fans could sense the sea change in the side. Peter Collins recalls: "In the 1960s there was no question that we were starting to slide. Things were just not right. The team was losing far too often, attendances were going down and the end of the maximum wage meant, for the first time, differences in the pay. Players wanted more than a nice place to live when they considered which club to sign for. Throughout the decade there was a gradual decline. We could no longer attract the players."

In 1961-62, the player who most personified Blackpool in the 1950s and whose name alone could bring the crowds flocking, finally departed. Stanley Matthews rejoined Stoke City from where he had been signed 15 years before. It was the end of an era.

He had played only two games in the campaign and his final match was a 3-0 defeat at Arsenal. It was a disappointing conclusion to an extraordinary Blackpool career, but at least the week before, more than 24,000 of the Bloomfield Road faithful had seen the maestro take his final bow at the ground that saw much of the best of the winger. It was a day of glory with a 4-0 win and the centre-forward Charnley profiting from those famous crosses with a hat-trick and Peterson collecting the fourth.

The only remnant from the glory days was Bill Perry, who had played in the 1953 Cup Final win. Father Time was catching up on the winger as well, and after a cartilage injury limited his first-team appearances, he departed in the summer of 1962 to nearby Southport. Perry remembers: "I was one of the last of the old team to leave Blackpool. I started getting problems with my knee and it spelt the end of my career. I had cartilage trouble and my knee used to swell up after every game. I knew when I left that the best was behind Blackpool. The quality of the players coming through was nothing like those who were there in the 1950s. Particularly in the forwards. Blackpool had the cream of the players in the League. We were all internationals. By the 1960s there just wasn't the money to buy that calibre of player or pay their wages."

With his playing days over, he rarely ventured back to Bloomfield Road. Not because he had turned his back on the club but, as he says, an ex-player often makes a poor spectator who spends too much of the time wishing he was out there performing. Rather than sit frustrated watching Blackpool drift towards football obscurity, he preferred to spend his time on the golf course and admits that like many footballers he caught the golfing bug. He went to a handful of Blackpool games each season in the 1960s but generally he monitored the fall from power of the once great Blackpool club in the sports columns of the newspapers.

Perry added: "The decline had been gradual with the good players starting to drift away and the replacements were not of the same calibre. There were not enough good up-and-coming players at the time. That was the neglect that happened during the early 1960s and was worse after about 1962 or 1963. The scouting system in Scotland under Vic Hamilton had been good and a steady stream of players had been sent down, but then that started to dry up. That was another reason the problems started."

Unlike other clubs, Blackpool had not developed a good youth set-up. Nor had its training facilities moved on to match the likes of, say, neighbouring Burnley, which had a vast scouting network and the impressive Gawthorpe training facilities where young players could be nurtured. In the past, Blackpool had been such a desirable location and the club was so successful in acquiring players that this was never a problem. The best performers were more than happy to produce their magic on the Bloomfield Road stage. Times had changed and the club had not been quick enough to read the runes and adapt. With insufficient funds to buy established stars, and without the structure to bring on talented youngsters, the future was always going to be bleak. As the on-field performances slumped, the crowd numbers fell and the revenue was reduced, thus exacerbating an already difficult situation.

There was, at least, the chance of Cup glory in the 1961-62 season. Not in the FA Cup where Blackpool departed at the first hurdle, beaten 2-1 in a replay at The Hawthorns after West Brom had held them to a goalless draw at Bloomfield Road. Yet in the second season of the League Cup they managed to reach the semi-finals. In the early rounds Port Vale, Leyton Orient and Workington were all accounted for and it brought a quarter-final tie against Sheffield United. A goalless draw at home made the Seasiders' task formidable, but they travelled to Yorkshire and won 2-0 with goals for Ray Parry and Ray Charnley.

In the early days of the competition, there was no Wembley trip for the winner. That was to come later. It was also a tournament that many leading clubs were ignoring so as not to burden their leading players with too many fixtures in a season. It has echoes of today and Sir Alex Ferguson with his policy of playing a largely Manchester United reserve side. But for diehard Blackpool supporters starved of success, a Cup win was still to be savoured. For others, though, the competition failed to ignite their enthusiasm. At the second round replay against Leyton Orient, the crowd had been just 6,098 and they missed a five-goal treat with Charnley getting a hat-trick and Parry two goals. Orient's only consolation was a solitary goal. For the semi-final, to be played over two legs,the Seasiders were drawn against Norwich City.

The lower division side countered Blackpool's attempts to play cultured football with direct and aggressive play, which brought its reward as they won 4-1 while enjoying less of the possession. They were helped by some casual defending that gifted the home side two goals. Former Blackpool man Derek Lythgoe opened the scoring in the 27th minute when, with Blackpool defenders appealing for offside, he calmly shot home. In the 49th minute, a pass from deep in defence found only the Canaries' Richard Scott and Blackpool were 2-0 down. Shortly after goalkeeper Bryan Harvey lost the ball and Jim Hill prodded it into an empty net. With eight minutes left Bill Punton had the strength to force his way past defenders for the fourth. Blackpool's only consolation was a goal for Peterson. It looked too big a deficit to pull back and so it proved with a 2-0 home win not quite good enough.

In the League, Blackpool finished 13th with the highlight being a 7-2 victory over Wolves in which Charnley scored four. Yet the last game of the season was to see the side's heaviest defeat when they travelled to The Hawthorns and lost 7-1. A Derek Kevan hat-trick in 25 minutes of the first half set the trend and although Blackpool tried to rally, they were too often let down by slack defending. It meant that the game turned into a rout with the only minor consolation being that Charnley's effort was the 30th League goal of the season for the centre-forward.

It was at this time that Francis Charlesworth, now the chairman of the Blackpool Supporters' Association, was allowed to go to matches on his own. He used to go on the Kop and it cost 1s 6d (8p), which, as he says, seemed a lot then but looks like good value today. He remembers there was no segregation of the fans and no trouble between rivals. Everyone was passionate about their team, but tribal loyalties did not spill over into violence. It would be the best part of a decade before crowd violence blighted the game.

He said: "The bigger and older I got, the further back on the Kop I used to stand. There was still a great atmosphere. Although the great players of the 1950s had gone, they were largely before our time. We didn't regard the visiting teams as anything special because we still saw ourselves as one of the elite sides. I probably hadn't even heard of some of the clubs in the Third and Fourth Divisions then. We still saw some great games and witnessed some impressive wins. We took it for granted that we would be playing the likes of Manchester United, Chelsea and Arsenal. I remember we once beat Arsenal 5-3 and that was a hell of a game. We were three up at half-time and Blackpool were cruising and it was like the old days. Unfortunately, in the second half they played more like the Blackpool of today and the Gunners came back, but we lifted our game and won."

The 1962-63 season saw another mid-table display with another 13th place finish in the League. Norwich City again proved the club's nemesis after their Football League Cup semi-final win the year before they accounted for the Seasiders in the third round of the FA Cup. Having been held to a 1-1 draw at Carrow Road, they travelled to Blackpool and enjoyed their day at the seaside, winning 3-1. In the League Cup, a tie against Manchester City needed two replays before the Maine Road outfit triumphed 4-2.

Charlesworth has particular memories of the Norwich City Cup game. He recalls that Blackpool had taken the lead and their equaliser came in controversial circumstances. A Norwich player shot and the ball went through the side netting of the goal and the referee didn't realise this and allowed the goal to stand. He believes the official should have checked the net properly before the start of the game. The players voiced their objections and so did the crowd, but it was no use. When he did inspect the hole, the ref seemed to accuse the goalkeeper of making it himself. The feeling on the terraces was that Blackpool had been cheated.

With the maximum wage gone and the attractions of the resort town paling in comparison to the money being offered by the big city clubs, Blackpool were beginning to struggle to attract players of calibre. Certainly there was not the personnel to take them to the top half of the table. When they did uncover talent, too often the pressing demands of the club's financial situation forced their sale. One player who emerged at this time, and was to be a star of England's World Cup win in 1966, was Alan Ball.

Ball had trials with Wolves and his local club Bolton, but he slipped through their net to the good fortune of Blackpool, who he joined in 1962. He was in the first team in August the same year. A skilful midfielder bursting with energy, that he stayed at Bloomfield Road for four seasons when bigger clubs were quickly queuing for his services was remarkable. For two seasons, in 1963-64 and 1965-66, he was the top goalscorer as they struggled. He made his England debut while at Blackpool in 1965 and went on to win 76 caps for his country. After the World Cup he went to Everton for a British record fee of £112,000 and then five years later broke the record again as he moved to Arsenal for £220,000. Perhaps a measure of his influence at the club is that the season after he left, the Seasiders slipped out of the top flight.

The future England captain was not the only player given his first-team chance at this time. There were other new faces appearing in the Blackpool line-up and these would be players who served the Seasiders well during the decade and beyond. Graham Oates was one, having signed as an apprentice in May 1961. The winger was kept largely on the sidelines with Bill Perry and Ray Parry still commanding first-team places, but by 1963-64 season he was a regular, although often troubled by injuries. He made 130 League and Cup appearances before departing for Grimsby Town in October 1968.

As the side underwent a major overhaul, another new name was John McPhee. He joined Blackpool from Motherwell in July 1962 for £10,000 and spent eight years with the Seasiders. He mainly played half-back but had something of a utility role at the club. Famed for his hard tackling and take-no-prisoners approach, he was never a dirty player. His approach to the game won him a great following on the terraces. He played nearly 300 League and Cup games for the club before departing in June 1970 for Barnsley. He ended his career at Southport.

The three seasons that preceded relegation in 1967 saw Blackpool slide perilously close to the drop with an 18th and 17th place finish in the League before a brief rally saw them reach the comparative safety of 13th. For the small-town Lancashire clubs the grim reality of football in the 1960s was being brought home. In 1963-64, attendances were down to an average of around 16,000, which was the lowest in the League. Manager Ron Suart was again the subject of the fans' wrath but survived. It was hard to see how anybody could have rescued the team from the position they were in, with insufficient money being generated through the turnstiles to compete in the market place, where transfer fees and wages were spiralling.

In 1963-64, Blackpool suffered a disastrous run, starting on November 23 with a 5-3 defeat away to Arsenal that took in the Christmas and New Year period and beyond without a win. In ten games they lost eight and drew two, with the worst reverse a 5-1 defeat against Chelsea at Bloomfield Road. By the last home game of the season, with Sheffield Wednesday the visitors, there were less than 13,000 spectators to witness a 2-2 draw. In the Cup it was the by now familiar story with another third-round defeat this time to West Brom in a replay at Bloomfield Road that was lost 1-0 after the side had battled to a 2-2 draw on their travels.

The following year it was more of the depressing same with another mid-season run that plunged the club into the doldrums. This time they went 14 games without victory, including nine defeats. Where once teams feared the Seasiders, now they were regarded as easy League points unless there was a major upset or they were playing fellow relegation fodder. In the Cup, the interest again did not last beyond the first match. This time it was Stoke City who triumphed 4-1.

A mini revival in 1965-66 merely delayed the inevitable. A new team was in place, with few of the old hands from earlier in the decade remaining. Jimmy Armfield still led the side and he had Tony Waiters in goal, who had been a rock throughout the decade. Up front Charnley and Leslie Lea had been regulars in the 1960s. Unfortunately for Blackpool, too many players coming into the side were journeyman pros, who might have frequently earned the admiration of the partisan home crowd but in truth struggled to cope with First Division football. When the Seasiders succeeded in attracting young talented players, they had difficulty keeping them. That applied to Alan Ball and to another player who would travel to Merseyside. This time to Anfield. The season saw the debut of Emlyn Hughes, who would play only 33 games before the 19-year-old was transferred to Liverpool for £65,000. The rest is history with his blossoming career bringing 62 England caps and domestic and European honours with Liverpool.

Some teams manage to linger on for years in the basement of the Premiership with each season bringing an inevitable relegation fight. So it had been for Blackpool in the old First Division as the club, once famed for the quality of its football produced by the internationals in its ranks, now relied on battling qualities to compete. Having struggled for most of the decade, the end was now in sight.

An Ignominious End

T HE end came for Blackpool in ignominious fashion with the sort of records achieved that make loyal fans cringe. The side managed to win only one game at Bloomfield Road all season and it represents the worst home record of any side in the history of the top division. The team's fortunes away from home were little better with five wins. The Seasiders did manage to beat both Liverpool and Everton, thus ensuring the curious distinction of having won more games on Merseyside than in Blackpool.

In the end, though, they managed only 21 points.

Francis Charlesworth recalls the way the season unfolded was grimly predictable. "From kicking the first ball at the start of the season, it seemed inevitable we were going down. We had just escaped by the skin of our teeth in so many earlier years that the fans were expecting the end to come. In the end it must have been one of the lowest points totals ever for the First Division. We were that bad and there were some heavy defeats. Many people were just amazed we had managed to stay up for so long. Sadly, many of the fans who stopped going in the relegation year never went back. We were awful."

Manager Ron Suart had pinned his hopes on a side that were frankly not good enough for the top flight. The cause was not helped by injuries, which meant it was rare for the same team to appear each week and 24 players were used throughout the season. Yet after 11 games in which the side's only points had come from two draws, there was a change of fortune that brought brief hope they might again escape the drop.

Syd Bevers was still a fanatical supporter, even though the Atomic Boys had long disbanded and consigned their tangerine and white suits to the attic or the back of the garage. He says: "Going to football was as natural to me as putting my coat on. I used to close my shop early to go to matches, that was how crazy I was. The relegation year was the culmination of a period that had been a dire struggle. The attendances were down as the defeats mounted. There was just poor performance after poor performance and it is hard to pick any matches out in the memory. We never seemed to be able to break out of the losing habit for long enough. It was disappointing although by that stage probably inevitable. Still, if I had my time again I would be just as committed to Blackpool. There have been good as well as bad times, but that season was one of the bad ones. When you're a football fan you can't pick and choose. It's a lifetime commitment, come what may."

A 3-1 win against Tottenham Hotspur was followed two days later with another visit to London for a third-round League Cup replay against Chelsea, which was also won 3-1. After what had gone before this was heady stuff indeed and 21,202 supporters were at Bloomfield Road for the visit of Newcastle United for a League match. The talk was of a new mood at the club and a huge boost to morale after the two previous wins. The form of Newcastle was ordinary with the North-East side having accumulated only ten points in the season.

The game was to be one of the few highlights in a season full of disappointment for Blackpool. Two players bought relatively cheaply by the standards of the day had outstanding games and there were hopes that Ian Moir and Alan Skirton could help prevent relegation. They both scored two in a six-goal demolition of Newcastle with the visitors failing to get on the scoreboard. It was Blackpool's biggest victory for nine years and an outstanding team effort. There were also goals for Ray Charnley and Jimmy Robson. As they made their way home, the delighted fans believed that now the Seasiders would begin a steady climb up the table.

The one name on their lips was that of Skirton, who for £65,000 had been signed from Arsenal where he had scored 53 goals in 145 League games. Previously he had been at Bath City and another of that club's old boys, and a Bloomfield Road legend, Stan Mortensen, had recommended him to Blackpool before the player's move to London. However, the outside-right was to stay for only three seasons before Mortensen, now the manager at Blackpool, sold him to Bristol City for £15,000. He was another who had become a popular figure with the local fans and they were sorry to see him go.

Two draws and two defeats in the next four games brought back a dose of reality and the results were never good enough to save the club. A 5-1 victory over Southampton on New Year's Eve, in which Charnley scored a hat-trick, gave hope that the dawn of 1967 might bring a change of fortune, but it was a temporary bright spot in a tide of general doom and gloom. Charlesworth was a big fan of the centre-forward. "He was a terrific header of the ball and although he was in a poor side, he used to bang them in consistently during the early 1960s. With the exception of Alan Ball, who was a quality player and it was amazing we kept him for so long, Charnley was definitely the best of a bad bunch. It was a very poor side."

The visit of Leeds United on March 25 began a six-match losing run that virtually sealed Blackpool's fate. The day before, they had defeated Chelsea 2-0 and, more in hope than anything, the fans prayed it might spark a revival. The first half ended goalless and Blackpool probably had the edge of the play, but it took only two minutes of the restart for Leeds to go ahead when Jack Charlton guided a Johnny Giles corner past Tony Waiters and it shattered the visitors' fragile confidence. As is often the case when results are going against a team, good fortune also seems to favour the opposition and although Blackpool tried hard, there was no goal for their endeavours. On the hour, the Seasiders' best chance fell to Charnley, who headed just over. With seconds remaining, Billy Bremner fired home a shot to put the issue beyond doubt.

It is the way with all football fans that they clutch at any straws, work out all manner of permutations, weigh up matches to be played and rivals faced, and they never finally give in until it is mathematically impossible for their side to be saved. With three matches left, though, Blackpool supporters were to be put out of their misery. The losing run was to end at Fulham, but the 2-2 draw the team earned was not enough. They were doomed to Second Division football for the first time since 1937 and the days of Matthews and Mortensen seemed a long way off. Yet again the Blackpool side were able to create chances, but as had been the failing all season, they were not able to convert them into sufficient goals. There was a feeling abroad that a proven goalscorer was needed if the club were going to make their stay in the lower league a brief one. The job of finding one now fell to old favourite Morty himself, who had returned as manager after the depressing results ensured the end for Ron Suart.

Before then there was the chance to sign off from First Division football at Bloomfield Road with their second home win of the season. The visitors were West Bromwich Albion and the sorely-tested patience of the local support ensured a crowd of only 9,986 were there to see the end. If they had hoped that with the pressure to climb clear of the relegation zone long since eased, the side would put on an exhibition display they were to be disappointed. West Brom had just scraped clear of relegation and had also sacked their manager, Jimmy Hagan, but they were to prove comfortable winners, 3-1.

The only bright spot was that the match marked the debut of a player who would become a favourite at Bloomfield Road. As Tony Green left the field he was given an ovation from the crowd despite the result. Green was Mortensen's first buy as manager and proved a real bargain, being signed for £15,000 while playing part-time football for Albion Rovers. The Glasgow-born player had only that one game in the relegation season, but stayed with the club until the 1971-72 season when he was sold to Newcastle United for a then club record of £150,000. He made his international debut while with Blackpool and in total won six Scottish caps, but serious injuries ended his career when he was still in his mid-20s and reaching his peak.

Peter Collins has seen all the players from the war years onwards and he says of Green: "For me he was the one who epitomised what you want in a footballer. He had good balance, all the skills, was a real crowd pleaser and was bursting with energy. I am convinced if it was not for his Achilles tendon problem he would have been the outstanding Scottish player of the post-war years. We used to get a lot of players from Scotland and even though the club was in decline, we were still at this time able to attract them and Green was as good as any. I would say he was one of the last to arrive at Bloomfield Road before the money took over and we couldn't compete any more."

He adds: "When we knew we were going down, everybody felt awful. The whole town was in mourning. We had been used to First Division football and being up there with the best in the land, and now for the first time since the 1930s we were down in the Second Division. A lot of things didn't go right during the season and with a decent rub of the green we might have survived. We went to Liverpool and won convincingly and that showed what the team was capable of, if everything went right, but it was all too late. We just hadn't been able to string a few good results together. We were unlucky not to come straight back the following year but we finished third and just missed out on goal-average."

Ray Charnley remembers: "The whole season was not very pleasant. That's all I can remember about it really. One game flowed into another and we just got into a losing run we couldn't shake out of. I think we had reached the stage where every season we were struggling and this was just the final chapter. There were one or two wins. We beat Newcastle, but there just weren't enough results went our way. "

His whole football career and subsequent life has been linked with the town. He first used to travel to the town from Lancaster by bus in his early playing days, then he moved to Blackpool and has lived there since. Ironically, he would earn more money at the end of his career with Preston North End, Wrexham and Bradford Park Avenue than he ever earned playing alongside Stan Matthews and company at Bloomfield Road. It was a measure of how the game had changed and the fact that the resort town could no longer challenge the best. The problems that beset the club then are still there now. Never again have Blackpool been able to compete.

He added: "We were relegated and my Blackpool career ended not long after a bad defeat at home to Millwall early the following season. I was proud of my record at Blackpool and it was always a thrill to score a goal. To be there when they were relegated was a bitter blow, but I had some great times at the club."

For their last game of the season, Blackpool travelled to Anfield to face Liverpool and remarkably they won 3-1. It meant a rousing end and that the campaign in the Second Division would start on a high note. The club would now join the ranks of Bolton Wanderers, Blackburn Rovers and Preston North End, who had all been relegated in recent years. Burnley would soon follow. The optimists hoped it would be a brief stay in the lower division before rebuilding would see the Seasiders return to the top flight.

Collins remembers another player who arrived in the relegation season and had hopes pinned on him that he could save the club from the drop. Alan Suddick had been spotted during Blackpool's 6-0 win over Newcastle, which can hardly have been the best advertisement given the season the Seasiders enjoyed. Still, the inside-forward repaid the £60,000 it cost Blackpool to sign him although he was to play most of his 340-plus games out of the First Division.

He became a great favourite and Collins still sees the player around town and enjoys a joke with him. He says: "I remind him he was hailed as the club's saviour when he arrived and we promptly got relegated. It was not the best start. We played West Ham United on Boxing Day and lost 4-1. He did, though, become a great favourite with the fans and like many others he still lives in the town. When you look at the good players we had, it's hard to imagine we got relegated. If we could have survived for a season while they settled in, we might have stayed up for a while. There was also Jimmy Armfield who was a great player for the club. I went to the same school as Jimmy and he was a right winger in those days. He is now an honorary vice-president at Blackpool but sadly, like me he won't live to see Blackpool flourish at the top again. It is an era that will never return. The best we can hope for is for the club to get back to a decent level of football."

An Ignominious End

The reality of football in the 1960s was brought home at the end of the relegation season with developments at another Lancashire club, which showed the way the game was going and the difficulties the small-town clubs would have to overcome if they were ever to compete. Manchester United won the title and confirmed their status as the country's number-one club. Matt Busby also announced that his club were prepared to spend £100,000 in the close season to further strengthen the squad. It was money way beyond the likes of Blackpool.

The Legacy and the Future

THERE has been little cause for celebration since the Seasiders slipped from the top flight and, unlike many of their fellow small-town Lancashire clubs who have enjoyed a revival in recent times, at the time of writing there is no sign on the horizon just yet of a change in fortune. While Blackburn Rovers, Bolton Wanderers, Burnley and their great rivals Preston North End are all enjoying Division One football and hoping the coveted Premiership place may not be long in coming, Blackpool are still languishing in the basement league.

Yet although the 1999-2000 season brought relegation, Francis Charlesworth is not the only one to believe there is now a buzz about the club. In the close season after the drop into Division Four, 2,500 season tickets were sold, which is no mean feat for a relegated side with a ground that has a 6,100 capacity, although improvements are under way. As Charlesworth wryly notes, there were plans submitted for a new stadium as early as 1935. It's been a long wait.

The off-the-field machinations that have so blighted the club since the 1960s now appear to have been put behind them. Blackpool has enjoyed more than its fair share of unwanted board-room interference, poor managerial appointments and hasty sackings of the man in the hot seat when he appeared to be doing a good job. The perilous financial position for much of the intervening years has only served to exacerbate the problem. All true supporters can only keep their fingers crossed and offer up a silent prayer that such problems are a thing of the past.

Hugh Kelly hopes that if Bloomfield Road is turned into a 26,000-capacity stadium, then there will be the people to fill it during the difficult next few years as rebuilding work is done on the pitch as well as off it. He hopes the shops, hotel and a night club being proposed as part of the development will help provide the money for the club to compete in the modern football world. At the moment he knows money at the club is tight.

At the memorial service to Stanley Matthews at the ground he was on the touchline for the minute's silence and his mind was cast back to the old days playing on the ground, and the memories from the golden era. It was not always as glorious as nostalgia may portray. He recalled some of the reality behind the sepia-tinted images: "When I came down in 1945 there was no football so we were put to work building the toilets. There we were, mixing three parts sand to one of cement. The latrines we built were still there at the service although they have now been demolished. Since then I've had a lot of happier memories on the old ground and hopefully those playing today will see some success and have their own fond thoughts about their time at the club."

The history since the club was relegated in 1967 has often been littered with 'if onlys'. The side managed by Stan Mortensen nearly bounced straight back at the first attempt in 1968 and fans well remember the excitement as a half dozen victories brought promotion within sight and confirmed the view of many that Blackpool would soon be back where they rightly belonged. A win at Huddersfield looked to have been enough to clinch a promotion place, only for Queen's Park Rangers to have triumphed at Villa Park with a last-minute own-goal that so cruelly denied Blackpool on goal-average.

Despite his popularity, as first a player and then a manager, Morty didn't last long with his contract being terminated by the board in April 1969, to the general horror of the town. He would not be the first former Bloomfield Road player to try to revive the fortunes of the club, but for all of them it was to be a largely forlorn battle. Allan

Brown would twice have spells at the club in the late 1970s and early 1980s. So too would one of the club's greatest players, Alan Ball, whose 12-month tenure was generally reckoned a disaster. There were many others whose reign was short and largely inglorious.

Too often in the years since the 1960s, a shaky financial situation has been compounded by poor direction from either manager or board and sometimes both. There has been the occasional high spot to keep the fans' interest and invariably flatter to deceive that the Seasiders could return to the elite. There was one season back in Division One after they won promotion in 1970. It was to be a brief flirtation as they were relegated the following season, winning only four games. They have never returned. There was the welcome diversion of European competition with the Anglo-Italian trophy in the summer of 1971, which was won with a 2-1 victory over Bologna after extra-time. They reached the Final of the same competition in the following year, only to lose to AS Roma.

The end of the 1970s saw Blackpool in the old Third Division and three seasons later, in 1981, they were relegated to the Fourth. They have yo-yoed between the two bottom divisions since. There have been trips to Wembley but only for play-off games to try to escape from the bottom two divisions. For most of the time since their demise they have been a 'selling' club, relying on discovering and nurturing talented youngsters, only to cash in as they attracted the attention of bigger and richer clubs. Even so, the finances were precarious enough for the local council to consider becoming involved and at one stage there were fears that the ground could be demolished to make way for a supermarket.

With the dawn of the new millennium there are hopes that off-the-field fortunes may have changed. They may have been waiting since the glory days of the 1950s for improvements to Bloomfield Road, but at long last there are significant developments in that area. There is a sense that those in charge of the club's financial affairs are committed to achieving change. The loyal fans who still crowd into the old ground are confident that the journey up the Football League is about to begin. The first steps are likely to be the hardest on the road to football enlightenment.

In the 1970s, the supporters' club folded and was revived as an independent association five years ago to try to get a better deal for supporters. Two years ago the association became the official supporters' club. Charlesworth said it was a measure of how the chairman, Karl Oyston, was doing a really good job and had been willing to listen to the views of the grassroots support. He thinks much of the enthusiasm among supporters in the town stems from a feeling that Oyston has the club going in the right direction on and off the field.

There are likely to be limits, though, on how far Blackpool can realistically hope to rise. Charlesworth is still a committed fan and is pleased with developments at the club, but he is a realist. He said: "While I enjoyed listening about the old days when I was younger, and longed to see Blackpool back as the greatest team in the country, I finally realised that the day would never come. I think the best we could hope for over the next decade is the top half of the First Division."

Since he began watching the team in the early 1960s, he has seen a sorry saga unfold. "I suppose I started watching them at the wrong time. I just saw the best before the decline set in. We have been going downhill gradually for many a year, not only on the field but with the state of the stadium, the owners we have had, declining attendances and the arrival of players who seemed to regard Blackpool as a retirement home in the twilight of their careers. They like the idea of finishing their career here because it is a nice place to live, there are good houses and top nightclubs."

He hopes the arrival of bulldozers at Bloomfield Road, preparing for a new stadium on the site, is a reflection of a general change of attitude at the club. It will not just be parts of the old ground swept away, but many of the old attitudes and problems that have dogged the club. With relegation in 1999-2000, he believes many in the town have realised that Blackpool FC is at rock bottom and there is even a danger the club could go out of the League completely.

With his involvement in generating support, he hopes more people who move to the town will come and watch the Seasiders, even though their first allegiance might be elsewhere. When the club are at the bottom is when fans should really be getting behind their team. During the relegation season the average attendance was under 5,000. There is, though, a large away following. The people who still watch Blackpool are fervent in their following. The supporters' branch in London, for example, has more than 200 members. It would be easy to switch allegiance to a winning side like Manchester United, but none would dream of doing it. Certainly those like Charlesworth, who have childhood memories of the Matthews swerve and the giant Scot, George Farm, in goal are hooked for life.

Ray Hall still goes and although the crowd is small, the supporters are vociferous and partisan. The old rivalry with Preston North End is still there, he notes. "North End always get a mention and some of the fans are obsessive about them. I think we should be more positive, but old habits die hard. It is a measure of the following we have that almost as many can turn up for an away game as at home. The same people still go to the same spot each week and you all meet up. I'm still a season ticket holder and what I notice most is that many of our fans seem to have come from everywhere but the town. When we play Preston or Burnley, their fans are all from the local towns, but I suppose it is the nature of Blackpool with so many people moving away and others coming to live here."

He adds: "While I can never see us in the Premiership the only way from here is up. Selling our best players hastened our demise and it is still a problem. We tend to sell one good player and buy three crap ones. We end up with has-beens and never-weres. I think a measure of the problems we face is reflected in my son who is a Manchester United supporter. Like many in the town he can't relate to how splendid it was here once and how famous we were. You walk around town now and all you see is Manchester United shirts and I despair. I think many of these people will come back to their football roots if they are given something to cheer."

Allan Brown still sees the team regularly and he believes relegation in 1999-2000 was a blow to the club. It means another big step to climb in the bid to get to a respectable position in the League and it is a hard task the club faces. "I think if they can get things sorted out off the field, they will progress. I've seen quite a few games and there is not a great deal of difference between the Second and Third Divisions. Looking at the teams in both, there is not a lot to choose. If they can get a little bit of luck they will hopefully get out of the basement. Whether you are at the top of the pile or the bottom, you always need a few breaks to make the difference."

Peter Collins still does work at the club in the commercial department and helps with the hospitality for corporate clients on match days. He believes that for the first time in many years, the organisation off the field is now looking good. The ground improvements will mean a stadium fit for football in the new millennium and on the field the team is assembling some useful players within the limitations of the money available for wages and transfers.

He added: "I can see the future being good here, but I'm only too aware that football has an unfortunate habit of kicking you in the teeth just when you think everything is coming right. We have had our share of bad luck over the years. There can be one or two incidents that are out of anybody's control and can change a game. As a fan they are the time when you feel really sick. There is nothing you can say, certainly there is nobody to blame. You just can't believe it is happening. Missing out on goal-average in the first season in the Second Division in 1968 was one such time. There have been many other times since when it appears the hand of fate has it in for Blackpool. This club will survive and it will bounce back. Being a committed fan, I know about taking the bad times with the good. We had plenty of celebrations in the 1950s, but we have had more than our share of reverses since."

Among the lows were relegation to the Third Division in 1978 for the first time in the club's history, when in the March they were in mid-table before winning only one of the last 16 games; going down to the Fourth Division in 1981 with former hero Alan Ball in charge; having to apply for re-election to the Football League in 1983; and losing a Fourth Division play-off match to Torquay United on penalties.

His ambition is to walk the streets of the town and see local youngsters wearing the tangerine strip of Blackpool rather than the latest Premiership fad. When that happens, he knows the club will have turned the corner and be on the way back. The days will return when the fortunes of the team will make or break the fans' weekend. A win and everyone is on a high. Defeat and it doesn't make for a pleasant Sunday. Bringing the passion for the club back to the town is the aim, and Collins for one believes they will succeed.

While Jock Dodds made a stand in the post-war years because he did not believe players were getting a fair deal, he feels the pendulum has now swung too far the other way with the amounts of money players earn and their lack of loyalty to their clubs. However, he certainly would like to play in the modern game where two or three years football can guarantee a lifetime's security, given the wages being paid. One aspect of the modern game he doesn't like is the bullying of referees. As he says, they are paid next to nothing to be threatened by players like Roy Keane of Manchester United who is on £50,000 a week. Keane is not the only one and there are many others as culpable.

Dodds has been a regular spectator at Bloomfield Road and believes things are looking up. The new chairman, Karl Oyston, has, he thinks, the right ideas for the club and the commitment to put them into practice. Indeed, he believes every Blackpool supporter owes the Oyston family a debt of gratitude because he fears without their intervention the club would have been doomed and the famous old ground reduced to a building site years ago.

For the immediate future, Dodds thinks promotion to the Second Division could easily be achieved. The team has one or two good players and the difference in standard is not that marked. As befits a centre-forward, he would like to see them acquire a proven goalscorer. What the long-term future will bring he is unsure, but a move out of the Third Division is the first priority.

While he thinks football in the old days was more exciting, he is not so blinkered that he doesn't appreciate what is played today. As well as watching most of Blackpool's home games, he sees the Premiership and European games on television and is impressed with the standard of football. The rash of imports he has mixed views about. On the one hand they raise the standard of the game and play some wonderful football. But they also prevent home-grown youngsters from getting a chance at the highest level which ultimately must be bad for the game.

With the Atomic Boys now a distant memory, Syd Bevers is still a regular at Bloomfield Road and has been a shareholder since 1960. Football has taken up a large part of his life and brought many happy times. Now, though, he thinks the only hope for the future is to recruit a magician from one of the shows on the piers. All Blackpool needs, he reasons, is a new team and a new ground – and it will take a magician to conjure that up. Without the help of magic, he thinks it will be a long haul over a number of years to claw their way back up the divisions. How far they can realistically go he is unsure.

As regards modern football, he is appalled at the huge transfer fees being paid, often for foreign players, and the astronomical salaries they can command. He bemoans the lack of home-grown talent. In his day, the Matthewses and Armfields were to be found in this country but it appears their successors are not. There are other changes. He says that modern crowd behaviour would make it impossible for the Atomic Boys to go through their routine nowadays. The risk would be too high. While in his day rival fans used to enjoy seeing the Atomic Boys and would give them a good ovation, he fears the reception would be more hostile from the gangs who now follow football.

There has been one appearance by Syd Bevers in orange gown and turban in modern times. At the age of 73, the man who confesses he has a weakness for publicity was persuaded to take to the pitch once more with the duck by the then chairman, Owen Oyston, in September 1987 for a League Cup-tie against Newcastle United. Oyston had seen the Atomic Boys in his youth and was hoping the presence of Syd might again bring luck to the team as they faced Newcastle United. When Syd protested that he was too old, the chairman told him that he was never too old and, thus encouraged, Syd found the outfit in the garage, dusted it down and stepped out once more. For fans of a certain generation it brought back memories of Blackpool's greatest days. Whether inspired or not, Blackpool won 1-0, although in the two-legged tie they were heavily beaten a fortnight later on Tyneside.

The days of the Atomic Boys are gone for ever and only the most wildly optimistic supporter can envisage a return to the new-look national stadium to witness a modern day Blackpool player emulating Harry Johnston and lifting the FA Cup. Yet a nucleus of committed fans have stood by the side through good and, increasingly in recent times, bad days, and their loyalty deserves some reward. With a major overhaul at the club it is to be hoped that they are not waiting too long. If the days of the Premiership may be a good way off, then a realistic ambition must surely be a return to the First Division. Then perhaps the old derby games with Bolton, Burnley, Blackburn and, of course, Preston North End, will again be eagerly-awaited fixtures.

Index

Kelly, Hugh 9, 22, 30, 32, 34, 50, 57, 63, 72, 76-77, 82, 84, 89, 92, 97-98, 106, 108, 111, 122, 141
Kelly, Jim 90
Kelsey, Jack 72
Kenilworth Road 107
Kevan, Derek 103, 128
Lampe, Derek 103
Lancaster City 22, 105
Langton, Bobby 48, 77
Law, Denis 123
Lawton, Tommy 48
Lea, Leslie 131
Leake, Albert 87
Leeds United 25, 42, 85, 102, 123, 135
Leicester City 120
Leith Athletic 26
Leyton Orient 127
Limerick 41
Lincoln City 21
Lisbon 48
Liverpool 45, 58, 74, 86, 110, 112, 131-133, 137-138
Lochee Harp 58
Lofthouse, Nat 48, 76-77, 110
Logie, Jimmy 71
Luton Town 26, 58, 86, 101, 104, 107, 113
Lytham 31, 63
Lythgoe, Derek 128
McFarlane, Alex 111
McGrory, Bob 52, 54
McIntosh, Jim 31
McIntosh, Willie 26, 58

McPhee, John 130
Madame Tussauds 42
Maine Road 61, 73, 89, 97, 123, 129
Manchester Central 111
Manchester City 89, 93, 97, 102, 123-124, 129
Manchester United 7, 13, 15, 25-26, 29-30, 33, 36-37, 45-46, 57, 59, 61, 63, 69-70, 86, 90, 92-93, 97-98, 107, 112, 120, 122, 127, 129, 139, 144, 146
Mannion, Wilf 48
Mansfield Town 61
Matthews, Jack 50
Matthews, Sir Stanley 7-8, 11, 13-14, 19, 21, 24, 26-28, 31, 34, 38-49, 51, 53-59, 63, 65-68, 71, 75, 77, 79-81, 83, 87-88, 92, 94, 97, 102-104, 108, 112-113, 120-121, 137, 141
Mayfair Hotel 35
Mercer, Joe 73
Merrick, Gil 62
Middlesbrough 22, 37, 58
Milburn, Jackie 66-67
Millwall 70, 138
Moir, Ian 134
Moir, Willie 78, 84
Molineux 44, 46, 86
Morecambe 104-105, 117
Morris, Johnny 34
Mortensen, Stan 14, 16, 21-23, 26, 32, 34, 38, 48, 51, 57, 61, 63-64, 66, 70, 73, 78, 81, 88,